The Essential Financial Toolkit

Also by Javier Estrada

FINANCE IN A NUTSHELL: A No-Nonsense Companion to the Tools and Techniques of Finance

The Essential Financial Toolkit

Everything You Always Wanted to Know About Finance But Were Afraid to Ask

Javier Estrada
IESE Business School, Barcelona, Spain

palgrave
macmillan

First published 2011 by
PALGRAVE MACMILLAN

Palgrave Macmillan in the UK is an imprint of Macmillan Publishers Limited, registered in England, company number 785998, of Houndmills, Basingstoke, Hampshire RG21 6XS.

Palgrave Macmillan in the US is a division of St Martin's Press LLC, 175 Fifth Avenue, New York, NY 10010.

Palgrave Macmillan is the global academic imprint of the above companies and has companies and representatives throughout the world.

Palgrave® and Macmillan® are registered trademarks in the United States, the United Kingdom, Europe and other countries.

ISBN: 978–0–230–28359–6 hardback

This book is printed on paper suitable for recycling and made from fully managed and sustained forest sources. Logging, pulping and manufacturing processes are expected to conform to the environmental regulations of the country of origin.

A catalogue record for this book is available from the British Library.

A catalog record for this book is available from the Library of Congress.

10 9 8 7 6 5 4 3 2 1
20 19 18 17 16 15 14 13 12 11

Printed and bound in Great Britain by
CPI Antony Rowe, Chippenham and Eastbourne

Contents

Preface

I have been lecturing executives in executive-education programs for many years now. The audiences are almost always heterogeneous both in terms of age and nationality, and, more importantly, in terms of background and training. Over time, I think I have learned to talk to the "average" participant in a program, without boring those that know some finance and without leaving far behind those that have little or no idea about it.

Part of the reason I have achieved this has to do with having provided participants with some background readings before the beginning of a program. The goal of the readings is to bring those without training in finance up to speed, which is valuable on at least two counts. First, those that do have some training in finance do not get bored with discussions of basic tools; and, second, it liberates precious time to focus on issues more central to the program. The ten chapters of this book were born as independent notes written for these very reasons.

As happens to many authors, after failing to find something that would fit what I needed, I decided to write it myself. And the characteristics I had in mind for the notes I was about to write were the following:

- They should be short; busy executives do not have either the time or the patience to read very many pages to prepare for an exec-ed program.

- They should be engaging and easy to read; otherwise, executives may start reading them but quit after a couple of pages.
- They should illustrate the concepts discussed with real data; most people do not find hypothetical examples very stimulating.
- They should cover just about all the essential topics; that would give me the ability to apply concepts such as mean returns, volatility, correlation, beta, P/Es, yields, NPV, IRR, and many others without having to explain them.
- They should answer many questions the execs would ask if I were discussing those basic topics with them; hence the Q&A format reflecting many of the questions I have been asked over the years when lecturing on those topics.

With these characteristics in mind I wrote a few notes and started assigning a couple before each program and sometimes another couple during the program; and, to my surprise and delight, many execs asked me for more. Many wanted similar notes discussing this or that topic not covered in the notes available, so I wrote a few more. Over time, I kept revising and hopefully improving all the notes. And, finally, I thought it was about time to revise them one last time and to compile them in a book, which is the one you are holding in your hands.

Many of these notes have also become useful to (and, I think, popular among) my MBA and executive MBA students. They find the notes short, easy to read, and instructive; and I again find them instrumental in freeing class time that can be allocated to other topics.

The chapters of this book do not assume or require any previous knowledge of finance; as long as you more or less remember your high-school math, you should be able to understand them just fine. Most of the topics discussed are basic and essential at the same time; a couple are a bit more advanced; and all of them are hopefully useful to you.

Each chapter is as self-contained as possible. The discussion in one chapter may occasionally refer to a concept introduced in a previous one, but it should be largely possible to jump into any chapter and understand it without having read the previous ones. The appendix at the end of the book discusses some useful Excel commands, restricting the scope to those related to the financial tools and concepts covered in this book.

Writing a book may feel like an individual effort but that is never really the case. Without encouragement from audiences and potential readers, without their comments and suggestions, and without an additional pair of eyes double-checking the many numbers and calculations that go into the next ten chapters, this book would have not been possible. For these reasons, I want to thank all my MBA students, executive MBA students, and participants in many and varied exec-ed programs. I also want to thank Gabriela Giannattasio for most efficiently checking every number, formula, calculation, and table in painstaking detail. And although this book would have not been possible without all this help and encouragement, I am obviously the only one to blame for any errors that may remain.

I both learned and had fun when writing this book. And I do hope you enjoy reading it at least as much as I enjoyed writing it. If you read this book, find it useful, and think it was worth your time, then it certainly will have also been worth mine.

JAVIER ESTRADA
Barcelona, Spain

Tool 1
Returns

This chapter discusses the concept of returns, essential for evaluating the performance of any investment. We will start by defining the arithmetic return in any given period and then expand the definition to multiperiod returns. Then we will define the logarithmic return in any given period and again expand the definition to multiperiod returns. We will conclude by discussing the distinction between these two types of returns.

Witty Professor (WP): Today we'll begin our short course on essential financial tools. Hopefully by the time we're done you'll have mastered many concepts that you may have found obscure and intimidating before.

Insightful Student (IS): Do you mean that by the end of the course we'll be able to tell one Greek letter from another?!

WP: Hopefully you'll learn that and a lot more. Yes, we'll talk about alphas, betas, rhos, and sigmas, but surely more important than the Greek letters are the concepts behind them.

IS: I find math more intimidating than Greek letters, and finance seems to be all about math.

WP: Not necessarily. Finance does use a lot of math, but the truth is that in order to master many essential and widely used concepts you don't need any more than high-school math and a few interesting examples.

IS: Great! When do we start then?

WP: Right now. The first thing we'll do is to make sure you understand how to calculate the return of an investment, both in any given period and over more than one period. And once we're done with that, we'll discuss an alternative way of calculating returns.

IS: Why do we have to calculate returns in two different ways?

WP: You don't *have* to calculate returns in two different ways. But there are in fact two definitions of returns, and because both are important we'll discuss both and we'll highlight when one is more appropriate than the other. OK?

IS: OK, but please don't complicate our lives unnecessarily!

WP: I won't. And assuming you believe me, let's start by taking a look at Exhibit 1.1, which we'll use as the basis of our discussion. As you can see, the exhibit shows the year-end stock price (*p*) of General Electric (GE)

Exhibit 1.1

Year	p ($)	D ($)	R (%)	r (%)
1997	24.46	0.35	–	–
1998	34.00	0.40	40.6	34.1
1999	51.58	0.47	53.1	42.6
2000	47.94	0.55	–6.0	–6.2
2001	40.08	0.64	–15.1	–16.3
2002	24.35	0.72	–37.5	–46.9
2003	30.98	0.76	30.3	26.5
2004	36.50	0.80	20.4	18.6
2005	35.05	0.88	–1.6	–1.6
2006	37.21	1.00	9.0	8.6
2007	37.07	1.12	2.6	2.6

over the years 1997–2007 in the second column and the dividend (D) the company paid in each of those years in the third column. Now, before we get down to specific numbers, a general question: If you buy a share of stock and hold it for one year, what are the potential sources of returns?

IS: That's easy, you get capital gains and dividends.

WP: Good. But let's define capital gains and tell me why you call them gains. Are they guaranteed to be gains?

IS: No, of course not. If I hold a share for one year, between the beginning and the end of the year its price can move up or down. If the price goes up I get a capital gain, and if it goes down I get a capital loss. If we look at your Exhibit 1.1, in 1999 GE delivered a capital gain and in 2000 it delivered a capital loss. Does that answer your question?

WP: Yes, but I have another one. How do you measure those capital gains or losses?

IS: You can do it in dollars, or euros, or any other currency. And you can also do it in percentages, which usually makes more sense.

WP: Why?

IS: Because it is obviously not the same to get a $10 capital gain from a stock for which I paid $100 a share as for one for which I paid $1 a share.

WP: Good! And now for the dividends. You said before that capital gains were not guaranteed because if a stock price goes down you get a capital loss. What about dividends? Are they guaranteed?

IS: Nope. Some companies pay them, and some companies don't. Some companies may have never paid them and suddenly start paying them, and some others may have always paid them and suddenly suspend them. Right?

WP: Right! And tell me, how is a dividend different from a dividend yield?

IS: A dividend is measured in dollars, or euros, or any other currency. And a dividend yield, which is just the dividend relative to the price paid for the share, is measured as a percentage.

WP: Right again! So let's get down to the numbers now. If you had bought GE stock at the end of 1997 and sold it at the end of 1998, what would have been your return?

IS: That's easy. I would have gotten a capital gain of $9.54, which is the difference between $34.00 (the price at the end of 1998) and $24.46 (the price at the end of 1997), plus a dividend of $0.40. That's a total gain of $9.94, which, relative to the $24.46 price I paid for the share, would have given me a 40.6% return.

WP: Fantastic! I want to make sure we generalize that idea so that we can calculate the return in any period. Let's define then the **arithmetic return (R)** as

$$R = \frac{p_E - p_B + D}{p_B} , \qquad (1)$$

where p_B and p_E denote the price at the beginning and at the end of the period considered, and D denotes the dividend received during that period. So, formally, the return you very properly calculated for 1998 would be expressed as

$$R = \frac{\$34.00 - \$24.46 + \$0.40}{\$24.46} = 40.6\% .$$

The numbers in the fourth column of Exhibit 1.1 show the returns of GE stock during the 1998–2007 period calculated this way.

IS: Quick question. Given your expression (1), can we say that $(p_E - p_B)/p_B$ is the capital gain or loss and D/p_B is the dividend yield?

WP: Exactly. And let me add that, technically speaking, the return we just calculated, which most people would simply refer to as "return," is formally called *arithmetic return* or *simple return*.

IS: But you said before that there was another way of computing returns, right?

WP: Yes, but before we get to that, two things. First, let me stress that if all you want is to calculate the change in the value of a capital invested over any given period, expression (1) is all you need; you don't really need the other definition of return. Second, before introducing any other definition, let's think how, with this definition, we can calculate returns over more than one period. How would you do that?

IS: Oh, you got me there. How would you do it?

WP: Well, it's quite simple. Let me give you the general expression first. If you want to calculate the return of an investment over a period of T years, you do it with the expression

$$R(T) = (1 + R_1)\cdot(1 + R_2)\cdot...\cdot(1 + R_T) - 1 , \qquad (2)$$

where **$R(T)$** denotes the **T-year arithmetic return** and R_t the arithmetic return in period t, the latter calculated in each period with expression (1).

IS: I think I understand, but just in case can you give us an example?

WP: Sure. Let's say you bought GE stock at the end of 1997 and you sold it at the end of 2007. The fourth column of Exhibit 1.1 shows the annual arithmetic returns, each calculated with expression (1). Using expression (2), then, the 10-year arithmetic return over the 1998–2007 period is

$$R(10) = (1 + 0.406) \cdot (1 + 0.531) \cdot \ldots \cdot (1 + 0.026) - 1$$

$$= 85.9\% \, .$$

IS: That's actually pretty easy.

WP: It is. And it really is all you need to know to calculate the return of an investment over any number of periods. And just to make sure you understand this, let me ask you: If you had invested $100 in GE at the end of 1997, how much money would you have by the end of 2007?

IS: That's easy. I'd have

$$\$100 \cdot (1 + 0.406) \cdot (1 + 0.531) \cdot \ldots \cdot (1 + 0.026)$$
$$= \$100 \cdot (1 + 0.859) = \$185.9 \, ,$$

right?

WP: Right! And now that you mastered everything you need to know about arithmetic returns, both over one period and over more than one period, let's consider the other way of calculating returns.

IS: Do we really have to?!

WP: No, we don't *have* to. Like I said before, if all you want is to calculate the change in the value of a capital invested between any two points in time, you'll be just fine with the arithmetic return. Still, the other definition of return comes up often in finance, so let's briefly discuss it.

IS: OK, it looks like we have no choice, so we'll bear with you a bit longer!

WP: Good. And you'll see that it's really simple. Let me give you the formal definition first. A *logarithmic return (r)*, or log return for short, is simply defined as

$$r = \ln(1 + R) \,, \tag{3}$$

where "ln" denotes a natural logarithm. So, remembering that we had already calculated the arithmetic return of GE in 1998 (40.6%), all it takes to obtain the log return is to simply calculate

$$r = \ln(1 + 0.406) = 34.1\% \,.$$

And that's it! No big deal, as you see. But just to make sure you understand this, you may want to calculate a few log returns for GE. And once you're done, check your numbers with those on the last column of Exhibit 1.1, where you can find the annual log returns of GE stock over the 1998–2007 period.

IS: I understand the calculation, but I'm not sure I understand the intuition behind the 34.1%.

WP: That's alright. For now keep these two things in mind: First, that it is exactly the same thing to say that in the year 1998 GE delivered a 40.6% arithmetic return as to say that it delivered a 34.1% log return. And, second, that another name for a log return is *continuously compounded return*.

IS: Understood. But what about multiperiod log returns? How do we calculate those?

WP: Rather easily, actually. If you want to calculate the return of an investment over a period of T years using log returns, you do it with the expression

$$r(T) = r_1 + r_2 + ... + r_T, \tag{4}$$

where $r(T)$ denotes the **T-year logarithmic return** and r_t the log return in period t, the latter computed in each period with expression (3).

IS: That's easy! I can even calculate myself that the 10-year log return of GE stock over the 1998–2007 period is

$$r(10) = 0.341 + 0.426 + ... + 0.026 = 62.0\% .$$

WP: Good! And since you're so smart, tell me: If you had invested $100 in GE at the end of 1997, how would you calculate, using log returns, the amount of money you'd have by the end of 2007?

IS: That's easy too. All I have to do is to multiply $100 by the sum of the log returns between 1998 and 2007, right?

WP: Gotcha! Not really. That's the only slightly tricky part. Using log returns, to calculate the ending value of a \$100 investment after T periods you have to calculate

$$\$100 \cdot e^{r_1} \cdot e^{r_2} \cdot \ldots \cdot e^{r_T} = \$100 \cdot e^{(r_1 + r_2 + \ldots + r_T)} = \$100 \cdot e^{r(T)},$$

where $e = 2.71828$. Note that these three expressions are just different ways of expressing exactly the same thing. And in my specific question, these expressions turn into

$$\$100 \cdot e^{0.341} \cdot e^{0.426} \cdot \ldots \cdot e^{0.026} = \$100 \cdot e^{(0.341 + 0.426 + \ldots + 0.026)}$$

$$= \$100 \cdot e^{(0.620)} = \$185.9,$$

which is, of course, the same number we had calculated before using arithmetic returns.

IS: Oh, you did get me there, but I understand now. It's actually not difficult. But I'm still a bit lost about why we need to bother with log returns. Aren't arithmetic returns enough?!

WP: It's natural to be a bit confused the first time you hear this, so don't worry about it. And let me give you an analogy that might just help to clarify things a bit. Suppose someone asks me about the distance between Miami and Chicago. If that someone is an American, I'd give her the distance in miles; if she were Italian, I'd give her the distance in kilometers. The distance, of course, is the same, but I can express it in two different ways. Does that ring a bell?

IS: It does! What you're saying is that if I start a period with $x and finish it with $y, I can measure that change either using arithmetic returns or log returns. The value of my investment will have changed by the same amount, but I can express the change in two different ways, right?!

WP: Right! And now that you're following me, let's push the analogy. If I give you a distance in miles, you simply multiply by 1.6 and get the distance in kilometers; and if I give you a distance in kilometers, you simply divide by 1.6 and get the distance in miles. Similarly, you can go between arithmetic returns and log returns by using the expressions

$$r = \ln(1 + R)$$

$$R = e^r - 1 \, .$$

So, as we said before, it is the same thing to say that during 1998 GE delivered a 40.6% arithmetic return as to say that it delivered a 34.1% log return. Using the two expressions above you'd get

$$r = \ln(1 + R) = \ln(1 + 0.406) = 34.1\%$$

$$R = e^r - 1 = e^{0.341} - 1 = 40.6\% \, .$$

IS: I follow you.

WP: Good. So you may also want to know that when changes are small, as, for example, when we measure them over a day, the arithmetic and log returns are very close; and when changes are large, as, for example, when we measure them over a year, these two types of returns may differ quite a bit from each other.

IS: Can you give us an example?

WP: Sure. Suppose that over one day your investment goes from $100 to $102, and over one year it goes from $100 to $150. You tell me, what are the arithmetic and log returns in both cases?

IS: In the first case, R = ($102 − $100)/$100 = 2% and r = ln(1.02) = 1.98%, so you're right, they're pretty close. And in the second case R = ($150 − $100)/$100 = 50% and r = ln(1.50) = 40.55%, so right again, they're pretty different.

WP: Good! So now you know just about everything there is to know about returns, both over any given period and over more than one period. Any final questions?

IS: Yes! I'm still not clear why we need to bother with log returns!

WP: Fair question. And, let me stress again, if you're only interested in measuring the change in the value of a capital invested over any given period, you'll be just fine with arithmetic returns. Stick with those. In fact, throughout this course, if we talk about "returns" without being any more specific, we'll mean arithmetic returns.

IS: I think I'll do just that.

WP: Hold on, let me give you two reasons for not dismissing log returns. First, they are widely used in financial theory. You may not care too much about that, but many models widely used in practice are derived from theory using log returns. And, second, they are behind the calculation of widely used financial magnitudes. For example, the calculation of volatility and correlations, concepts that we will explore in the near future, is usually based on log returns; the reasons for this are more statistical than financial, so I won't bore you with them. In short, then, arithmetic returns are used for most practical purposes, and log returns are largely used "in the background" of many important practical calculations. Does that answer your question?

IS: It does! I think I'm pretty much on top of the different ways of calculating returns. I can't wait for the second discussion.

WP: Coming up!

Tool 2
Mean Returns

This chapter discusses three definitions of mean returns and highlights their different interpretations and uses. In many cases, particularly when evaluating risky assets, the concept of "mean return" is meaningless, and stating the type of mean return discussed, arithmetic or geometric, is essential. Also, when investors trade actively, their mean return and that of the asset in which they invest may differ substantially, which requires yet another concept, the dollar-weighted mean return.

Witty Professor (WP): Having explored the concept of periodic returns in our last session, today we'll focus on summarizing the information of a time series of returns. Suppose I give you the returns of an asset over a long period of time. Looking at them, or often even making a graph, will not help you much in assessing the asset. What you'd have to do is to summarize the information contained in those returns into two numbers, one for return performance and the other for risk.

Insightful Student (IS): Does it have to be just one number for return performance and one for risk?

WP: Good question. And the answer is "no" on at least two counts. First, there is, as we'll discuss today, more than one way of summarizing the return performance. And, second, there are many and varied ways of summarizing risk.

IS: So today we'll focus on characterizing the "good" side of the coin, return performance, and leave the "bad" side of the coin, risk, for some other session?

WP: Yes. And we'll start easy, with something you know from your high-school days, which is taking averages.

IS: That's pretty easy.

WP: It is. But although calculating a simple average of returns is both easy and widely done in finance, the resulting number is often misinterpreted. So, let's start by taking a look at Exhibit 2.1, which contains the year-end stock price of Sun Microsystems over the years 1997–2007 in the second column and the corresponding annual returns in the third column.

IS: Just to clarify, those returns are what in our previous session we called arithmetic or simple returns, right?

WP: Yes, and because Sun paid no dividends during this period, those returns are simply the capital gain or loss that Sun stock delivered each year. For the year 2007, for example, the –16.4% return is simply calculated as ($18.13 – $21.68)/$21.68.

Exhibit 2.1

Year	P ($)	R (%)
1997	19.94	–
1998	42.81	114.7
1999	154.88	261.8
2000	111.48	−28.0
2001	49.20	−55.9
2002	12.44	−74.7
2003	17.88	43.7
2004	21.56	20.6
2005	16.76	−22.3
2006	21.68	29.4
2007	18.13	−16.4

IS: Got it. So you were saying that we need to somehow aggregate those returns to come up with a number that summarizes the return performance of the stock.

WP: Yes, and one way of aggregating those returns is to simply take their average. So let's define the **arithmetic mean return (AM)** as

$$AM = (1/T) \cdot (R_1 + R_2 + ... + R_T) , \qquad (1)$$

where R_t denotes the simple return in period t and T denotes the number of periods (or, what's just the same, the number of returns). And, given this definition, let me ask you, what is the arithmetic mean return of Sun stock over the 1998–2007 period?

IS: That's easy, it should be

$$AM = (1/10) \cdot (1.147 + 2.618 + ... - 0.164\%) = 27.3\% .$$

WP: Correct. And what do you make out of that number?

IS: Well, that seems easy too. If Sun stock delivered a 27.3% arithmetic mean return over the 1998–2007 period, then if I had invested $100 at the end of 1997, I should have found myself with $100·$(1.273)^{10}$ = $1,116.8 at the end of 2007, right?

WP: No! That's a typical confusion, and it's precisely what the arithmetic mean return is *not*!

IS: How come? I don't understand.

WP: Well, you remember from our last session how to calculate multiperiod returns, right? So, if we had started with $100 at the end of 1997 and obtained the annual returns shown in Exhibit 2.1, then we would have ended 2007 with

$$\$100 \cdot (1 + 1.147) \cdot (1 + 2.618) \cdot ... \cdot (1 - 0.164) = \$90.9 \,!$$

IS: Wait a minute! How come we have a positive arithmetic mean return and we end up with *less* money than we started with? Something's wrong here!

WP: Yes, what's wrong is what you think the arithmetic mean return indicates. So, let's start with what it does *not* indicate. An arithmetic mean return does *not* tell you the rate at which a capital invested evolved over time. In the example we're considering, the 27.3% arithmetic mean return does *not* tell you that your $100 increased at the annual rate of 27.3%.

IS: So, what you're saying is that if we read somewhere that an asset had an arithmetic mean return of, say, 10% over the past 20 years, we should not necessarily conclude that we could have made money on that asset during that time.

WP: Exactly! We may or may not have made money. Look, here's a simple example. Suppose you invest $100 in an asset. In the first year the price goes up by 100%, and in the second year it goes down by 50%. How much money do you end up with?

IS: Well, that's easy. At the end of the first year, after the 100% return, I'd have $200; and at the end of the second year, after the –50% return, I'd have $100.

WP: That's right. And what is the arithmetic mean return over these two periods?

IS: It's just the average of the two returns, so that's $(1/2) \cdot (1.00 - 0.50) = 25\%$. You're right! The arithmetic mean return is 25% and yet I ended up with just as much money as I started with!

WP: And what do you make out of that?

IS: Well, simply that, as you said before, the arithmetic mean return does not indicate the rate at which a capital invested evolved over time. I got that. But what does it indicate then?

WP: It indicates at least two things. First, given that returns fluctuate over time, some are high, some low, some positive, some negative, the arithmetic mean return simply tells you, looking back, the average return over the period considered.

IS: Well, it's always useful to know the average return of an asset, particularly when comparing across assets. But what's the other interpretation?

WP: Well, the other interpretation is a bit tricky. Under some conditions, the arithmetic mean return is, looking ahead, the most likely return one period forward.

IS: But that doesn't look very tricky. What you're saying is that if we had to forecast the return of Sun stock in 2008, we would predict 27.3%, right? What's the problem with that?

WP: Well, I wish it were that simple. I don't want to get into muddy waters here, so let me just say that if the returns of the asset considered fulfill certain statistical conditions, then the arithmetic mean does happen to be the most likely return, and when that's the case it may be a reasonable prediction of the return one period ahead.

IS: And what's the problem with that?

WP: Simply that it's not always the case that the returns of the asset considered fulfill these conditions. But you don't want me to get into statistical discussions, do you?

IS: No, not really!

WP: Well then, let's move on and consider another way of calculating mean returns.

IS: Why do we need another?

WP: Simply because if you ask different questions you're likely to get different answers! If you ask what has been the average annual return of Sun stock over the 1998–2007 period, then 27.3% is the right answer. And if you ask what is the most likely return of Sun stock for the year 2008, then 27.3% *may* be the right answer, depending on those statistical issues we're waving our hands on.

IS: So?

WP: So that if you ask at what rate a capital invested in Sun stock evolved over the 1998–2007 period, then, as you realized yourself before, the arithmetic mean return is not going to give you the right answer.

IS: OK, different question, different answer, I get that.

WP: Good. Let me then introduce the ***geometric mean return (GM)***, which is given by

$$GM = \{(1 + R_1) \cdot (1 + R_2) \cdot ... \cdot (1 + R_T)\}^{1/T} - 1 . \qquad (2)$$

IS: That looks a bit more difficult than the arithmetic mean return.

WP: Just a bit, so let's make sure that we understand both how to calculate and interpret this magnitude. Let me start by asking you, then, what is the geometric mean return of Sun stock over the 1998–2007 period?

IS: Let's see, it should be

$$GM = \{(1 + 1.147) \cdot (1 + 2.618) \cdot ... \cdot (1 - 0.164)\}^{1/10} - 1$$

$$= -0.9\% \,.$$

WP: Good. And how do you interpret that number?

IS: Well, given the hints you've been dropping here and there, I suspect that this is the annual rate at which a capital invested in Sun stock evolved over the 1998–2007 period. Which actually means that we lost money at an annual rate of almost 1% a year.

WP: Exactly. Does that explain why, if you put $100 in Sun stock at the end of 1997, you ended up with less than $100 by the end of 2007?

IS: It sure does. I started the year 1998 with $100, lost money at the average rate of almost 1% a year over 10 years, and ended up, as we calculated before, with $90.9. Or, more formally, $100 \cdot (1 - 0.009)^{10} = \$90.9$. And now that I take another look at Exhibit 2.1, given that Sun paid no dividends and that the stock price is lower at the end of 2007 than it was at the end of 1997, I should have guessed from the start that investing in Sun stock during this period would have led me to lose money.

WP: Right again. I see you're following me, so let me first tell you that if you ever heard the term "mean compound return" before, that's exactly what a geometric mean return is: a mean return, compounded over time. And now let me ask you another question. In the case of Sun stock over the 1998–2007 period, we have a positive arithmetic mean return and a negative geometric mean return. Will that always be the case? All assets, all periods?

IS: I suspect not, but I really don't know.

WP: Your suspicion is correct. It is indeed the case that, for any given asset and period, the arithmetic mean return is always larger than the geometric mean return.

IS: Always? No exceptions?

WP: Just one, and it's irrelevant as far as financial assets are concerned. In a time series in which all returns are the same, the arithmetic mean return and the geometric mean return are also the same; in all other cases, the first is larger than the second.

IS: Does that mean that, as I had mistakenly done before, if I compound a capital invested at the arithmetic mean return, I will always end up *overestimating* the terminal capital?

WP: Exactly. And if the difference between the two means is large, as in the case we've been discussing, then you can substantially overestimate the compounding power of an asset. Remember that you first thought that $100 invested in Sun stock at the end of 1997 would turn into $1,116.8 by the end of 2007, when what really happened is that you ended up with $90.9! That's quite a difference, isn't it?

IS: It is!

WP: That's why it's always important to make sure that you know what type of mean returns are being discussed. If I just tell you that the "mean return" of Sun stock over the 1998–2007 period was 27.3%, I'm not lying to you. But you should not rush to calculate $\$100 \cdot (1.273)^{10} = \$1,116.8$ and conclude you could have made a bundle of money. You should first ask me whether that "mean return" is arithmetic or geometric.

IS: And I should always compound a capital invested at the geometric, not at the arithmetic, mean return.

WP: Exactly.

IS: But in the case of Sun stock, the difference between the arithmetic and the geometric mean return is huge. Is the difference always that large?

WP: No, not necessarily. In fact, it depends on the volatility of the asset. The more volatile the returns of the asset, the larger the difference between the arithmetic and the geometric mean return.

IS: Which means that, when considering volatile assets such as hedge funds, internet stocks, or emerging markets, just talking about "mean returns" makes little sense, right?

WP: Right again!

IS: But can you give us a little perspective? We see that the difference between the two mean returns in the case of Sun is very large, but not all assets are so volatile. What is a typical difference between these two magnitudes?

WP: There is really no such thing as a typical difference. It really does depend on the asset you're considering, and, as you can see in Exhibit 2.1, Sun did treat its shareholders to quite a wild ride over the 1998–2007 period. But take a look at Exhibit 2.2, which shows the long-term (1900–2000) arithmetic and geometric mean return for a few international stock markets. As you can see, the difference between these two magnitudes is in some cases large and in some cases not so large.

IS: That's illuminating. In the case of Sun we've been discussing, the difference between the arithmetic and the geometric mean return is over 28 percentage points, but in the case of the US and the UK stock markets it's under 2 percentage points. And what we should make out of that is that the returns of Sun stock are far more volatile than those of the US and the UK stock markets, right?

WP: Exactly. And now that you seem to have grasped the difference between these two ways of calculating mean returns, let's introduce a third one.

IS: A third definition of mean returns?! Why do we need so many?

Exhibit 2.2

	Canada	France	Germany	Japan	UK	USA
AM (%)	11.0	14.5	15.2	15.9	11.9	12.0
GM (%)	9.7	12.1	9.7	12.5	10.1	10.1

Source: Adapted from Elroy Dimson, Paul Marsh, and Mike Staunton, *Triumph of the Optimists: 101 Years of Global Investment Returns*, Princeton, NJ: Princeton University Press, 2002.

WP: If you ask different questions, you're likely to get different answers, remember?

IS: Maybe we should stop asking questions then!

WP: Well, the point is that there is another interesting question you could ask regarding mean returns. Suppose you had invested some money in Sun stock during the 1998–2007 period. What if I asked you what was the mean annual return *you* obtained?

IS: We already discussed that. I would have obtained a mean annual compound return of –0.9% over those 10 years and would have then turned each $100 invested into $90.9.

WP: That's correct, but you're implicitly assuming something that does not reflect the behavior of all investors.

IS: And what's that?

WP: Well, you're implicitly assuming that you bought shares at the end of 1997 and that you passively held them through the end of 2007, at which point you sold them. In that case, you're right, your return and the return of Sun stock are identical.

IS: And what's wrong with that?

WP: Nothing at all. But not all investors follow such a passive strategy. Some buy and sell over time. What if after buying, say, 100 shares of Sun at the end of 1997, you would have then bought another 100 shares at the end of 2000, and finally sold the 200 shares at the end of 2007? What would have been your return then?

IS: Oh, you got me there. But it seems to me that the 100 shares bought at the end of 2000 at $111.48 each were not such a great investment given that by the end of 2007 Sun was trading at only $18.13.

WP: Your intuition is correct. The second column of Exhibit 2.3 shows the same prices of Sun stock we've been discussing. Now, take a look at the third and fourth columns. The third column shows that you bought 100 shares at the end of 1997, another 100 shares at the end of 2000, and that you sold the 200 shares at the end of 2007. And, given the share price at those times, the fourth column shows that you took $1,994 out of your pocket at the end of 1997, another $11,148 at the end of 2000, and finally put $3,626 into your pocket at the end of 2007 when you sold the 200 shares.

IS: So what you're saying is that instead of calculating the mean return of Sun stock over the 1998–2007 period,

Exhibit 2.3

Year	p ($)	Shares-1	CF-1 ($)	Shares-2	CF-2 ($)
1997	19.94	+100	−1,994.0	+100	−1,994.0
1998	42.81	0	0.0	0	0.0
1999	154.88	0	0.0	0	0.0
2000	111.48	+100	−11,148.0	0	0.0
2001	49.20	0	0.0	0	0.0
2002	12.44	0	0.0	+100	−1,244.0
2003	17.88	0	0.0	0	0.0
2004	21.56	0	0.0	0	0.0
2005	16.76	0	0.0	0	0.0
2006	21.68	0	0.0	0	0.0
2007	18.13	−200	+3,626.0	−200	+3,626.0

we need to calculate *my* mean return over that period, right?

WP: Right. And can you see why these two mean returns may differ?

IS: I think so. If I had bought shares at the end of 1997 and sold them at the end of 2007 and had not made any transaction in between, then my mean return and that of Sun stock *must* be the same. But if I had made one or more transactions anywhere in between, there is no reason why my mean return and that of Sun should still be the same.

WP: And why's that?

IS: Because my return will depend not only on the price of Sun stock at the end of 1997 and 2007 but also on the prices I paid and received when I bought and sold during that period.

WP: That's exactly right. What we need to calculate, then, is your ***dollar-weighted mean return (DWM)***, which, to tell you the truth, has a bit of a scary expression so I won't even write it.

IS: But without the expression how can we calculate the number?

WP: We'll get to that in a minute, but for now remember that this is a course of basic financial tools and therefore we're trying to stay away from fancy financial formulas as much as we can. In any case, have you ever heard about the concept of internal rate of return?

IS: The IRR! It does ring a bell! Is it the return a company gets from investing in a project?

WP: Pretty close. A bit more precisely, an internal rate of return, or IRR, is the mean annual compound return a company gets from a project, considering all the cash put into it, and obtained from it, over time.

IS: That sounds pretty much like what we've been discussing about my investment in Sun stock. I take $1,994 out of my pocket at the end of 1997 to buy 100 shares; then $11,148 at the end of 2000 to buy another 100 shares; and finally put $3,626 into my pocket at the end of 2007 when I sell the 200 shares. So the question is what has been my mean compound return given all the cash that came in and out of my pocket, and given the times at which that cash flowed in and out.

WP: Exactly! That mean compound return is precisely the dollar-weighted mean return, which at the end of the day is nothing but the internal rate of return of the cash flows resulting from investing in an asset.

IS: And in the case we've been discussing, what is the dollar-weighted mean return? And, just as important, how can we calculate that number?

WP: Let's start with your first question. The dollar-weighted mean return that results from buying 100 shares of Sun stock at the end of 1997, another 100 shares at the end of 2000, and finally selling the 200 shares at the end of 2007 is –16.0%. A pretty bad return, as you can see, and much worse than the return of Sun stock. Can you see why?

IS: I think so. Like I suggested before, buying 100 shares at the end of 2000 at over $111 and selling them at the end of 2007 at just over $18 doesn't sound like a great deal! So the decision of buying those second 100 shares was made at a really bad time, and that lowers my mean return relative to that of Sun stock.

WP: That's exactly right. But since you're telling me that your –16.0% dollar-weighted mean return was lower than the –0.9% geometric mean return of Sun stock, let me ask you: Can it be the other way around? Is it possible that your dollar-weighted mean return is higher than the geometric mean return of Sun stock?

IS: Well, if my lousy return is due to the fact that I bought at a bad time, I guess that if I buy at a good time then my return could be higher than that of Sun stock, right?

WP: Right! And to confirm that, just take a look at the last two columns of Exhibit 2.3. The next-to-last column shows that this time you bought 100 shares at the end of 1997, another 100 shares at the end of 2002, and finally sold the 200 shares at the end of 2007. The last column shows that to buy the first 100 shares at the end of 1997 you took $1,994 out of your pocket; to buy the second 100 shares at the end of 2002 you took another $1,244 out of your pocket; and when you finally sold the 200 shares at the end of 2007 you put $3,626 into your pocket.

IS: And what would have been my dollar-weighted mean return?

WP: In this case, your dollar-weighted mean return, or mean (annual) compound return of your investment, would have been 1.4%, higher than that of Sun stock.

IS: Well, I understand that my dollar-weighted mean return can be higher or lower than the geometric mean return of the asset I invest in, but will you finally tell us how to calculate it?

WP: How about if I give you half the story?

IS: Why only half?

WP: Because after our ten core sessions there will be an additional optional session on some useful Excel commands, and I'd rather discuss your question at that time. So, for now, let me just say that, having agreed that a dollar-weighted mean return is nothing but the IRR of an investor's cash flows in the investment considered, if you know how to calculate an IRR in Excel, then you also know how to calculate a dollar-weighted mean return.

IS: That's pretty easy!

WP: It is. And for those who are not clear on this calculation, fear not, we'll discuss this issue by the end of the course. And now, having half-answered your last question, time to wrap up!

IS: Actually, after discussing three different definitions of mean returns, each devised to answer a different question, we do need a wrap-up!

WP: Here we go then: When summarizing return performance, the concept of "mean return" is far too ambiguous. There is more than one definition of "mean return," and each is devised to answer a different question. If you want to know the average return over a period of time, or (under some conditions) the most likely return for the next period, then you calculate the arithmetic mean return. If you want to know the rate at which a capital passively invested in an asset evolved over time, or the asset's mean compound return, then you calculate its geometric mean return. And remember that the difference between the arithmetic and the geometric mean return is increasing in the volatility of the asset, the former always being larger than the latter. Finally, if you want to know the mean compound return an *investor* obtained by following an active strategy, you calculate his dollar-weighted mean return, which is nothing but the internal rate of return of his cash flows in the asset considered, and that can be higher or lower than the geometric mean return of the asset. So, for today, like Bugs Bunny used to say, that's all folks!

Tool 3
Risk: Standard Deviation and Beta

This chapter discusses two very widely used definitions of risk, standard deviation and beta, both of which are at the heart of modern finance. Some say that risk, like beauty, is in the eyes of the beholder. Maybe it is, but even if that is the case, understanding the relationship between the standard deviation, beta, and risk is essential for anyone who wants to have a basic knowledge of finance.

Witty Professor (WP): Having discussed how to calculate periodic returns and how to summarize their perform-ance through mean returns, we now move our focus to the "bad" side of the investment coin: risk.

Insightful Student (IS): It was hard enough for us to learn two definitions of return and three definitions of mean return, are you sure you want to go over one other definition?!

WP: No, you're right. We won't go over *one* other defin-ition ... we'll go over *two* other definitions!

IS: Is there anything in finance that is defined in just one way?

WP: Well, the timing of your question is not very good because there are *many* competing definitions of risk. Today we'll explore the two most widely used.

IS: Let me guess, the reason we'll explore two definitions today is because if we ask different questions we're going to get different answers, right?!

WP: I see that you're beginning to learn some finance! That is exactly right. In this case, in fact, of the two definitions we'll explore, which one is more appropriate depends on the context in which an asset is considered. But I don't want to get ahead of my story.

IS: OK, so what's the first step then?

WP: The first step is to consider the numbers in Exhibit 3.1, which shows the returns of Johnson & Johnson (J&J),

Exhibit 3.1

Year	J&J (%)	GM (%)	S&P
1998	29.0	21.3	28.6
1999	12.5	25.7	21.0
2000	14.2	−27.8	−9.1
2001	14.0	−1.0	−11.9
2002	−7.9	−20.8	−22.1
2003	−2.1	52.9	28.7
2004	25.2	−21.5	10.9
2005	−3.4	−48.4	4.9
2006	12.4	64.0	15.8
2007	3.6	−16.4	5.5
AM	9.8	2.8	7.2

General Motors (GM), and the S&P-500 index (S&P) over the 1998–2007 period. Let's leave the index aside for the moment and focus just on the two stocks. So here's an easy question for you: Which one of the two stocks do you think is riskier?

IS: Are we supposed to know that? We haven't even defined risk yet!

WP: But that's part of the point. Given the returns in Exhibit 3.1, which stock would you consider riskier? I'm not asking you to give me a definition of risk; I'm just asking for your perception of the risk of these two stocks.

IS: Well, I'm sure that this is not a very technical way to look at it, but it seems to me that GM has delivered higher and lower returns than J&J. As Exhibit 3.1 shows, GM delivered returns above 50% in two of those ten years, and returns below –20% in four of those ten years. J&J delivered returns neither as high nor as low as did GM.

WP: Good. So let's elaborate on that. You perceive GM to be riskier than J&J because its returns were "more extreme," meaning very high and very low, or at least higher and lower than those of J&J, right?

IS: That's right.

WP: Now, take a look at Exhibit 3.2, which plots the returns of J&J and GM shown in Exhibit 3.1. Does the picture confirm your initial intuition that GM is riskier than J&J?

Exhibit 3.2

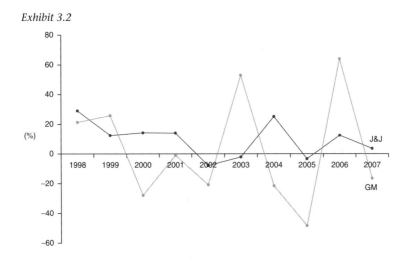

IS: It sure does! GM returns look like a roller coaster compared to those of J&J!

WP: Well, it turns out that one of the most widely used
magnitudes in finance formalizes your informal view
of risk.

IS: And what is that magnitude?

WP: It is the **standard deviation of returns (SD)**, which
is defined as

$$SD = \{(1/T)\cdot [(R_1 - AM)^2 + (R_2 - AM)^2$$
$$+ \dots + (R_T - AM)^2]\}^{1/2},\tag{1}$$

where R_t indicates the return in period t, AM the arithmetic mean return of the asset over the period considered, and T the number of returns in that period.

IS: Not so fast, that doesn't look very easy!

WP: I'm not rushing, don't worry. Let's think a bit about this expression. Note, first, that it considers the deviations between each return and the (arithmetic) mean return; that is, the farther away each return is from the mean return, the higher the standard deviation will be.

IS: Well, that makes sense; the more returns tend to depart from their mean, the more uncertainty we face, right? If we had two assets with a 10% mean return, one with returns clustered between 9% and 11% and the other with returns scattered between 1% and 19%, I'm sure we would all perceive the second asset to be riskier than the first.

WP: Exactly. Now, why do you think we square the differences between each return and the mean return?

IS: Oh, that's easy. If we didn't, then a return, say, 6 percentage points above the mean and another 6 percentage points below the mean would cancel each other out. So we'd be adding 0 to the calculation of the standard deviation even though both returns depart substantially from the mean return.

WP: Exactly! Very good! So, having considered all the departures between each return and the mean return, and having squared all these departures to avoid their cancelling each other out, expression (1) then shows that we take the average of all these squared differences.

IS: Well, that makes sense too; some of these differences will be high, some others low, so we want to get an idea of the average (squared) difference. But why do we take a square root?

WP: Well, think about it. If we just calculated an average of the squared differences between each return and the mean return, the resulting number would be some rather strange magnitude expressed in "percent squared."

IS: So we take a square root of a "percent square" in order to obtain a magnitude in percent?

WP: Exactly. And now that we understand the standard deviation a bit better, how about if we calculate it for J&J and GM stocks? And, very importantly, let's see if it reflects your intuition that GM is riskier than J&J.

IS: OK, so using the returns in Exhibit 3.1 and expression (1) we get

$$SD(J\&J) = \{(1/10) \cdot [(0.290 - 0.098)^2$$
$$+ ... + (0.036 - 0.098)^2]\}^{1/2}$$
$$= 11.5\% ,$$

$$SD(GM) = \{(1/10) \cdot [(0.213 - 0.028)^2$$
$$+ ... + (-0.164 - 0.028)^2]\}^{1/2}$$
$$= 34.9\% ,$$

so, yes, GM is a lot riskier than J&J!

WP: Great. So, having calculated these two numbers, and having seen that they confirm your intuition that GM is riskier than J&J, now tell me: How would you interpret the 11.5% and the 34.9%?

IS: Well, these numbers are the square root of the average squared deviation from the mean, right?

WP: Right. And in English?

IS: I see your point. I don't know. How would you interpret these numbers in a more intuitive way?

WP: Well, that's actually a bit of a problem with the standard deviation. The definition you gave is exactly right, and I can't do any better. That's why the best way to use the standard deviation is not so much by focusing on the absolute number but by thinking about it as a *relative* number; that is, 34.9% is a lot higher than 11.5%, and therefore GM is a lot riskier than J&J.

IS: Well, that seems quite easy.

WP: And it is in fact the best way to use the standard deviation as a measure of risk.

IS: But I seem to remember reading somewhere that it's also used to build some intervals, though I'm not sure how or what they're for. Can you explain that?

WP: Sure, but briefly and mostly to prevent you from making a mistake a lot of people make.

IS: What mistake?

WP: Well, some people would build an interval by adding and subtracting one standard deviation from the mean return and claim that the returns of the asset are expected to be within that interval with a probability of, roughly, 68%. Similarly, they'd add and subtract two standard deviations from the mean and claim that the returns of the asset are expected to be within that interval with a probability of, roughly, 95%. In the case of J&J stock, for example, they'd say that there's a 68% probability that the returns of J&J in any given year fall within the interval (–1.7%, 21.3%) and a 95% probability that they fall within the interval (–13.2, 32.8%).

IS: Well, that seem easy to understand. What's wrong with that?

WP: That the probability of obtaining returns in those intervals are accurate *only if* the returns of the asset you're considering fulfill some very specific statistical conditions. More precisely, they are accurate *only if* the returns you're dealing with are normally distributed. But, like I've asked you before, you don't want me to get into statistical discussions, do you?

IS: Not really, but can you at least tell us whether, in general, those intervals are accurate?

WP: No, I can't. The point is that unless you do know that the returns you're dealing with are normally distributed, and many people that use those intervals actually don't know whether that's the case, you should stay away from making those calculations.

IS: Gotcha. So, are we done with the standard deviation then?

WP: We're *almost* done; two more things to go. First, let me highlight that the standard deviation of an asset's returns and the *volatility* of the asset's returns refer to exactly the same thing. In other words, volatility and standard deviation are used in finance as interchangeable terms. And, second, we still need to think why we need another measure of risk, which brings me to the fact that the standard deviation is a measure of *total* risk.

IS: What do you mean by that?

WP: Well, so far we've been considering J&J and GM as individual assets. In other words, if we had all our money invested in one of the two stocks, then we would bear all the risk of that stock. But most people don't invest that way – most people diversify their portfolios. Can you guess why?

IS: Well, my grandmother used to say that if you put all your eggs in one basket and you drop the basket, you're in big trouble. But if you distribute your eggs among several baskets and you drop one, you'd still have the eggs in all the other baskets intact. Same with investing, I guess. If you put all your money in one stock and the stock tanks, there goes your whole portfolio too.

WP: Your grandmother was right, and so are you. Putting all your money in just one stock seems like a great thing to do when the stock is flying high, but it doesn't look that smart when the stock unexpectedly tanks. Think of all those Enron employees who had most of their money invested in Enron stock when it seemed the company could do no wrong; their big smiles were wiped off their faces pretty much overnight when the company went bankrupt.

IS: I understand all this, but what does it have to do with the standard deviation as a measure of risk?

WP: A lot actually, because if we consider one asset at a time, as if we were investing all our money on that asset, then we'd be bearing all its risk, which would then be properly captured by the standard deviation. But most people, most of the time, diversify their portfolios, and in that context the standard deviation is no longer an appropriate measure of the risk of each asset in the portfolio.

IS: Why not?

WP: Well, think about it. Suppose you have a widely diversified portfolio. On any given day, month, or year, a company may be hit with bad news and its stock price will fall. But, more likely than not, some other company in your portfolio will report good news and its stock price will rise. If you have many companies in your portfolio, a lot of the bad news and price drops will be offset by good news and price increases. In other words, part of the risk of each individual stock will cancel out part of the risk of some other stocks in your portfolio.

IS: So you're saying that if instead of holding just one asset we hold the same asset within a diversified portfolio we bear less than the total risk of the asset, right?

WP: Exactly. The part of the risk that is diversified away is usually called *nonsystematic* risk, or *idiosyncratic* risk, and consists of all those company-specific and industry-specific factors that affect the stock price of companies.

IS: But why can't we diversify *all* risk away?

WP: Good question. We can't because there are factors that tend to affect all companies in the same direction and at the same time. Think, for example, about interest rates; when they go up, everything else equal, all stock prices are pulled down. Much the same happens with many other macroeconomic factors and political events.

IS: Are you saying that although stock prices are affected by many company-specific and industry-specific factors that push some stock prices up or some others down, there are some economy-wide factors that pull all stock prices in the same direction?

WP: Exactly. And it's because these factors tend to pull all stocks in the same direction at the same time that we can't diversify away from them.

IS: I see. And how do we call this risk that can't be diversified away?

WP: It's called *systematic* risk, or *market* risk, and it's measured by a stock's **beta** (β).

IS: The famous beta! I've read and heard about it more than once, but I'm not quite clear about what it measures.

WP: It can be interpreted at least in two ways, but first let me stress that beta is a relevant measure of an asset's risk *only* when you hold the asset within a widely diversified portfolio. And, in that case, one way to think of an asset's beta is as the contribution of the asset to the volatility of the whole portfolio.

IS: Oops, I think you lost me there.

WP: That's OK. It's not the most intuitive way to think about beta, but I wanted at least to mention it. Fortunately, there is a much more intuitive way to think about it, and to discuss it we'll go back to our J&J and GM stocks.

IS: I hope you're not going to ask us to calculate the beta of each stock. I'd have no idea how to do that!

WP: Well, to tell you the truth, we won't even bother with formulas in this case. Betas are widely available, so you can always go to some public web page, like Yahoo Finance, and find the beta of just about any company. So I'll just tell you that the betas of J&J and GM are 0.25 and 1.35.

IS: And what do those numbers mean?

WP: In general, beta is the reaction of a stock to fluctuations in the market. And, a bit more precisely, it's the average return of a stock given a 1% fluctuation in the market. So J&J's beta of 0.25 indicates that when the market goes up or down 1%, J&J stock tends to go up or down, on average, 0.25%. And GM's beta of 1.35 indicates that when the market goes up or down 1%, GM stock tends to go up or down, on average, 1.35%.

IS: So you're saying that J&J stock tends to mitigate the market fluctuations, and that GM stock tends to magnify them, and therefore GM is riskier than J&J, right?

WP: That's right. A beta of 1 indicates average risk, or return fluctuations similar to those of the market; a beta higher than 1 indicates higher risk (larger return fluctuations) than the market; and a beta lower than 1 indicates lower risk (smaller return fluctuations) than the market.

IS: Can a beta be negative?

WP: Good question. In theory, yes; in practice, very rarely. If the period you look into is long enough, and if you focus on stocks with respect to the market in which they trade, or stock markets with respect to the world stock market, then betas are virtually always positive. Actually, can you guess why?

IS: Well, I guess that those economy-wide factors we discussed, pulling all stocks in the same direction at the same time, play a role, right?

WP: Exactly. Although all sorts of information pull some stock prices up and some others down, underneath all those influences the market factor pulls them all in the same direction. Or, put differently, although stock prices may fluctuate widely in the short term, in the longer term they tend to all go up together. And how they fluctuate on that way up, relative to the market, is precisely what beta captures.

IS: Now I finally understand the famous beta! And even at the risk of asking too much, given the goals of this course, can you at least give us a hint about how to estimate it?

WP: Again, betas are widely and publicly available, so you might as well stick to finding them rather than estimating them. But, if you insist, I'll go as far as saying that technically you need the covariance between the returns of a stock and the returns of the market, and the variance of the market's returns. Once you estimate those two, you put the first over the second, and there you'll have your beta. You can try this yourself with the numbers in Exhibit 3.1 if you wish.

IS: Maybe I'll try. But right now I'm more curious about the uses of beta. I understand it is a measure of systematic risk, a measure of an asset's risk when the asset is part of a widely diversified portfolio, and a measure of an asset's return fluctuations relative to those of the market. But if investors do hold diversified portfolios, and if in that case beta is the proper measure of risk, how can I use it to determine the returns I should expect from an asset?

WP: Very good question...but bad timing again! That's precisely the issue we'll discuss in our next session, which means that right now it's wrap-up time.

IS: Good! As usual, I think we do need a wrap-up!

WP: Here we go then: Risk can be defined in more than one way, though standard deviation and beta are the two magnitudes most widely used to assess it. The standard deviation or volatility measures an asset's total risk and is related to uncertainty; the higher this number, the less we can predict the future prices and returns of the asset considered. Beta, on the other hand, is a measure of systematic risk, that risk we can't get rid of even when we hold a widely diversified portfolio, and captures the reaction of a stock to fluctuations in the market. Some stocks amplify the market's fluctuations, and some others mitigate them, and we think of their risk accordingly. And now, time for a break!

Tool 4
Diversification and Correlation

This chapter discusses the issue of diversification, something that academics preach and most investors practice. It is often said that putting all the eggs in the same basket is not a good strategy. Diversification, at the end of the day, consists of following that simple advice when building investment portfolios, a process in which the correlation between assets plays a critical role.

Witty Professor (WP): We discussed in our last session two measures of risk, standard deviation and beta, and although my plan for today was to discuss the relationship between beta and required returns, I'm going to change that plan a bit.

Insightful Student (IS): Why?

WP: Because some of you wanted to discuss the concept of diversification a bit further, and so we'll do that today. And we'll postpone our discussion about the relationship between beta and required returns for our next session.

IS: Sounds good. I actually did have some doubts about the concept of diversification, particularly regarding the role of the correlation coefficient, which you didn't mention and I never seem to quite understand.

WP: That's a very common doubt, and we'll certainly talk about that today. But let's walk before we run, so let's first consider the returns of the three hypothetical assets on Exhibit 4.1. The exhibit shows their returns over 10 periods, as well as their arithmetic mean and standard deviation, both of which you know how to calculate by now.

IS: Yes, we do! So, what's the story with those three assets?

WP: Well, since diversification is all about combining assets into a portfolio, let's consider a combination between Assets 1 and 2. Let's assume that given whatever capital we have to invest, we put 13% of our money

Exhibit 4.1

Period	Asset 1 (%)	Asset 2 (%)	Asset 3 (%)
1	25.0	21.3	32.5
2	5.0	24.3	22.5
3	22.5	21.6	31.3
4	6.0	24.1	23.0
5	17.5	22.4	28.8
6	4.0	24.4	22.0
7	31.0	20.4	35.5
8	5.5	24.2	22.8
9	24.0	21.4	32.0
10	4.0	24.4	22.0
AM	14.5	22.9	27.2
SD	10.0	1.5	5.0

in Asset 1 and 87% in Asset 2. How would you calculate, period by period, the return of that portfolio?

IS: That's easy. For Period 1, for example, the return of the portfolio (R_p) would be

$$R_p = (0.13)(0.250) + (0.87)(0.213) = 21.8\%,$$

and the only thing that would change from period to period would be the return delivered by each asset.

WP: Great. Now, what do you think we would get if we do the same thing for the second period?

IS: I don't know, but we can just calculate it. The return of the portfolio in the second period would be

$$R_p = (0.13)(0.050) + (0.87)(0.243) = 21.8\%,$$

which is kind of funny; that's the same return as in the previous period!

WP: Well, it may be funny, but it's also right. And if you find that curious, let me surprise you: If you calculate period by period the return of a portfolio invested 13% in Asset 1 and 87% in Asset 2, you will find that the return of the portfolio, give or take a small rounding error, is always...21.8%!

IS: No way! You're cheating somewhere!

WP: I'm not. You can crunch the numbers yourself if you don't believe me, but let me save you some time. Take a look at Exhibit 4.2.

Exhibit 4.2

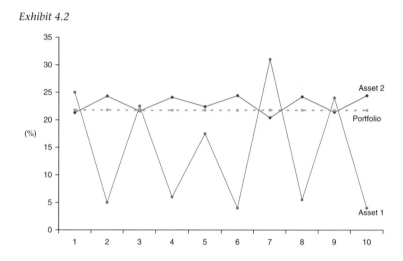

IS: I'm looking but I'm not sure I understand it.

WP: Well, the picture shows the returns of Assets 1 and 2 over the ten periods we're considering, as well as the return of the 13–87 portfolio. And, as you can see, the return of this portfolio is just a straight line at 21.8%.

IS: I can hardly believe it! We combine two risky assets and we end up with a riskless portfolio? What's going on here?

WP: Well, let's rule out cheating to start with! And, before I answer your question, let me ask you to consider another combination of assets. Consider now a portfolio invested 50% in Asset 1 and 50% in Asset 3. If we were to calculate the return of this portfolio over the ten periods we're considering, what do you think we would get?

IS: Please don't tell me that another portfolio with a riskless 21.8% return!

WP: Nope, quite different from that actually. Take a look at Exhibit 4.3, which plots the returns of Asset 1, Asset 3, and the 50–50 portfolio.

IS: That portfolio is far from riskless! It's actually pretty volatile!

WP: It is. And if you're wondering what determines that when combining Assets 1 and 2 we end up with a risk-less portfolio, and when combining Assets 1 and 3 we end up with a volatile portfolio, you're asking the right question. Can you guess what it all comes down to?

IS: No idea!

WP: To the correlation coefficient you have doubts about, so let's talk about that.

IS: Great! Let's see if I can finally understand what that coefficient is all about!

Exhibit 4.3

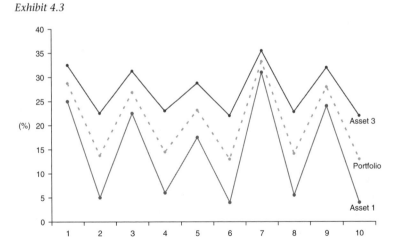

WP: It's actually fairly simple. The correlation coefficient is a magnitude that measures the sign and the strength of the relationship between two variables. When two variables tend to move in the same direction, this coefficient is positive; and when they tend to move in opposite directions, this coefficient is negative.

IS: That's pretty simple. But how do we know if the relationship is weak or strong?

WP: Formally speaking, the correlation coefficient can take any value between −1 and 1. In the first case, the two variables have a perfect negative relationship; in the second case, a perfect positive relationship.

IS: I understand that by a positive relationship you mean that the variables tend to move in the same direction and by a negative relationship that they tend to move in opposite directions. But what do you mean by a *perfect* relationship?

WP: I mean that in the extreme cases in which two variables have a correlation of −1 or 1, if I know the value of one variable, I can *exactly* determine the value of the other. If the correlation between any two variables x and y is -1, then they are linked by a relationship of the type $y = a - b \cdot x$; and if the correlation between them is 1, then they are linked by a relationship of the type $y = a + b \cdot x$. Then, in both cases, if I know x, I can exactly determine y.

IS: I see. So do you mean to say that the correlation coefficient measures the strength and sign of *linear* relationships?

WP: Strictly speaking, yes, although most people seem to forget this. A high and a low correlation are informally referred to as characterizing a strong and a weak relationship, although strictly speaking they characterize a strong and a weak *linear* relationship.

IS: So, let me see if I understand. A positive correlation indicates that two variables tend to move in the same direction; a negative correlation indicates that they tend to move in opposite directions; a correlation of −1 indicates that two variables are linked by a perfect, negative linear relationship; a correlation of 1 indicates that they are linked by a perfect, positive linear relationship; and in these last two cases, if I know the value of one variable, I can exactly determine the value of the other. Is that right?

WP: Perfectly correct!

IS: OK, but it seems to me that those correlations of −1 and 1 are rather hypothetical, aren't they? I mean, I cannot imagine any two financial variables that would be related in such a neat, perfect way.

WP: You're absolutely right. But understanding those extreme values is still useful, even if we don't expect to find financial variables that would be characterized by those extreme correlations.

IS: Why?

WP: Because for any two financial variables you may be interested on, the closer their correlation is to −1 or to 1, the stronger the (linear) relationship between them would be. On the other hand, the more their correlation departs from –1 or 1 and the closer it gets to 0, the weaker the (linear) relationship between them would be. And if their correlation is 0, there would simply be no (linear) relationship between them.

IS: So, given what you're saying, just by taking a casual look at Exhibits 4.2 and 4.3, we should be able to conclude that Assets 1 and 2 are strongly negatively correlated and Assets 1 and 3 are strongly positively correlated, right?

WP: Right! In fact, we can even make a stronger statement. The correlation between Assets 1 and 2 is exactly –1, and the correlation between Assets 1 and 3 is exactly 1.

IS: How do you know that?

WP: Well, I know because those assets are hypothetical, remember? So, when I came up with their returns, I made sure that those were the correlations between them. But, if you don't believe me, you can calculate the correlations and check for yourself.

IS: But you haven't told us how to calculate correlations!

WP: You're right. I'll say a couple of things about that later on but right now let me stress something very important that follows from Exhibits 4.2 and 4.3: *The lower the correlation between two assets, the more you gain by combining them.*

IS: Why's that?

WP: Well, we won't get into any math here, but I could formally show you that as long as two assets have a correlation of –1, you can always find a specific proportion of your money to invest in each asset so that you can completely eliminate the risk of your portfolio. And, as far as risk reduction goes, it obviously doesn't get any better than that!

IS: But you said before that a correlation of –1 is possible in theory but not really in practice, right?

WP: Right, but it's still useful to know what is the best-case scenario in terms of diversification, isn't it? It's useful to know that when two assets have a correlation of –1, you could always combine them in a very specific way so that you could eliminate completely the volatility of the portfolio, even if you can't find two assets with that correlation in practice. Similarly, it is useful to know that when two assets have a correlation of 1, there are no diversification gains from combining them.

IS: Why not?

WP: Well, think about it. If you form a portfolio with two assets that move in the same direction in a fully synchronized way, your portfolio will move in exactly that way. Just take a look at Exhibit 4.3 for confirmation. What's the gain from combining Assets 1 and 3?

IS: None. I see your point. You're saying that when two assets have a correlation of 1, there's nothing to gain from combining them; and when two assets have a correlation of –1, there's the most to gain from combining them. Then, it necessarily follows that the lower the correlation between two assets, the more diversification benefits we get from combining them, right?

WP: That's right. The closer we get to a correlation of 1, the lower the diversification benefits; and the closer we get to a correlation of –1, the higher the diversification benefits. And, importantly, make sure you avoid a common mistake: You don't obtain diversification benefits only when the correlation between two assets is negative; *you obtain diversification benefits as long as the correlation between two assets is lower than 1.* The lower the better, but even positive correlations, as long as they are lower than 1, produce diversification benefits.

IS: I think I'm beginning to understand the "mysterious" correlation coefficient!

WP: That's good, so let me make another important and related point. Whenever you combine two assets with a correlation equal to 1, the volatility of your portfolio will simply be the weighted average of the volatilities of the two assets in the portfolio.

IS: Wait! What do you mean by a weighted average?

WP: I mean that if we put 30% of our money in Asset 1 and 70% of our money in Asset 3, then the volatility of our portfolio (SD_p) would be

$$SD_p = (0.30) \cdot SD_1 + (0.70) \cdot SD_3,$$

where SD_1 and SD_3 denote the volatility of Assets 1 and 3. Similarly, if we put 60% of our money in Asset 1 and 40% in Asset 3, the volatility of our portfolio would be

$$SD_p = (0.60) \cdot SD_1 + (0.40) \cdot SD_3 ;$$

and the same for any other two weights.

IS: OK, got it. If we combine two assets with a correlation equal to 1, the volatility of the portfolio will simply be equal to the weighted average of the volatilities of the two assets in the portfolio. Please continue.

WP: Well, remember that a correlation of 1 was the worst-case scenario in terms of diversification. It then follows that as long as we combine two assets with a correlation lower than 1, then the volatility of the portfolio will be *lower* than the weighted average of the volatilities of the two assets in the portfolio.

IS: That sounds wonderful!

WP: Well, it's just the "magic" of diversification! As long as two assets are not perfectly, positively correlated, we can combine them, and the volatility of the resulting portfolio will be lower than the weighted average of the volatilities of the two assets in the portfolio. And, of course, the lower the correlation between two assets, the lower the volatility of the portfolio will be relative to the weighted average of the volatilities of the two assets.

IS: In other words, if our goal is risk reduction, the lower the correlation between two assets, the more we gain by combining them, right?

WP: That's exactly right, and it brings us to a very important point: Don't think of the correlation coefficient as some sort of statistical magnitude with little practical importance. It should be obvious from our discussion that this coefficient is *critically* important from a *practical* point of view. You can't really build a portfolio properly if you ignore the correlations between the assets in the portfolio.

IS: I fully agree with that by now. What I find a bit strange, though, is that we're only talking about diversification and risk reduction, but surely investors are interested in goals beyond risk reduction. Am I wrong about that?

WP: You're not; in fact, you're absolutely right. I framed the whole discussion in terms of risk reduction to avoid mixing different goals. So, let me ask you, what do you think would be other plausible goals for investors to have?

IS: Well, I can at least think of one other: To maximize returns for a desired level of risk.

WP: Very good, and here's the good news: Everything we said about the relationship between correlations and risk reduction applies to the relationship between correlations and return maximization for a desired level of risk. In short, the lower the correlation between two assets, the higher the returns we can get for a desired level of risk.

IS: What about risk-adjusted returns?

WP: What about them?

IS: Well, it seems to me that investors don't really want to just minimize risk; if they did, they'd put all their money safely in a bank, with 0 risk and a very low return; but most investors don't do that. On the other hand, it seems to me that investors don't really want to just maximize returns; if they did, they'd have their portfolios loaded with very risky assets such as internet stocks or emerging-markets stocks; but, again, most investors don't do that. So it seems to me that investors want the best balance between risk and return; they want the highest possible returns at every level of risk. Does that sound plausible?

WP: It's more than plausible: It's absolutely right. We will have a full session to discuss the issue of risk-adjusted returns, so without formally defining them now let me say this: Everything we said about the relationship between correlations and risk reduction also applies to the relationship between correlations and the maximization of risk-adjusted returns. In short, the lower the correlation between two assets, the higher the risk-adjusted returns we can get.

IS: And that means that the lower the correlation between two assets, the higher the returns we can get per unit of risk borne, right?

WP: Right again!

IS: I think I finally understand the correlation coefficient and its relationship to portfolio diversification!

But there's one thing I'd like to know a bit more about. You mentioned that correlations of −1 and 1 are hypothetical and not to be expected between financial variables. Can you give us some examples of actual, observed correlations?

WP: I sure can. Take a look at Exhibit 4.4, which shows the annual stock market returns of the USA, Germany, New Zealand, Norway, and the UK, over the 1998–2007 period. The returns of these five markets are given by the MSCI indices, in dollars, and accounting for both capital gains and dividends. As you can see from the last line, the US stock market is positively and strongly related to the stock markets of Germany and the UK, and positively but rather weakly related to the stock markets of New Zealand and Norway.

IS: I see. And the fact that all four correlations are positive indicates that the USA and all these four markets tend to move in the same direction, right?

Exhibit 4.4

Year	USA	Germany	New Zealand	Norway	UK
1998	30.7%	29.9%	−21.5%	−29.7%	17.8%
1999	22.4%	20.5%	14.3%	32.4%	12.5%
2000	−12.5%	−15.3%	−33.0%	−0.4%	−11.5%
2001	−12.0%	−22.0%	9.5%	−11.7%	−14.0%
2002	−22.7%	−32.9%	26.1%	−6.7%	−15.2%
2003	29.1%	64.8%	57.8%	49.6%	32.1%
2004	10.7%	16.7%	37.5%	54.5%	19.6%
2005	5.7%	10.5%	3.2%	25.7%	7.4%
2006	15.3%	36.8%	17.7%	46.3%	30.7%
2007	6.0%	35.9%	9.8%	32.4%	8.4%
Correlation	−	0.89	0.21	0.37	0.89

WP: Right. In fact, if you look over a long enough period of time, you will find that all stock markets tend to be positively correlated to each other. Although they may behave erratically individually and with respect to each other in the short term, in the long term they all tend to go up, which translates into positive correlations.

IS: So you're saying that all financial assets are positively correlated?

WP: No, that's a stronger statement than mine. I'm saying that if you look at several stock markets over a long period of time, they all tend to be positively correlated. Similarly, if you look at stocks within any given market over a long period of time, they all tend to be positively correlated. But that does not apply to all assets. Gold, for example, is known to have been negatively correlated to stock markets over some periods of time. Which actually explains why, when stock markets are weak, some people tend to buy gold; they expect gold to go up when stock markets go down. And although it hasn't worked like that all the time, it has worked like that some of the time.

IS: So, based on our previous discussion, gold would be an ideal addition to a portfolio of stocks, right? Because if most correlations between stocks are positive, but gold is negatively correlated with stocks, at least part of the time, then it would enable us to reduce risk a lot; or to enhance returns substantially for a desired level of risk; or to significantly improve risk-adjusted returns. Is that a fair statement?

WP: It is. In fact, even when the correlation between stocks and gold is not negative, it is positive but fairly low, in which case your previous statement is still true.

IS: I see we're running out of time, so I have one last question. Is it fair to say that investing in mutual funds is popular because they provide diversification?

WP: There are many reasons for buying mutual funds instead of individual stocks, but you're right, obtaining wide diversification at a low cost is one of the main reasons. Just think that by buying one share of a mutual fund, you're buying into a well-diversified portfolio of stocks in any industry, country, or region you may want exposure to.

IS: I see. And maybe one last question? What about the calculation of correlations?

WP: Well, I'm only going to go as far as saying that, as usual, Excel can do that for you in the blink of an eye. And, as I mentioned before, after we're done with our ten core sessions there will be an additional optional session on some useful Excel commands, so hold on to your question until then.

IS: Wrap-up time, then?

WP: Unless you want to spend your break between sessions in the classroom, yes! Here we go. Diversification is one of the cornerstones of modern financial theory. All smart investors should hold widely diversified portfolios because that's what enables them to maximize risk-adjusted returns. When diversifying portfolios, the correlations between assets play a critical role. The lower the correlations, the higher the diversification benefits; that is, the more we can reduce risk; or the more returns we can get for any desired level of risk; or the higher the risk-adjusted returns we can get. And since the show must go on, it will go on, but in our next session!

Tool 5
Required Returns and the CAPM

This chapter discusses the relationship between risk and return. It is obvious that investors would want a higher exposure to risk to be compensated with a higher return, but in order to estimate the actual return investors should require at different levels of risk, we need a model. The Capital Asset Pricing Model (CAPM), one of the models most widely used in finance, provides a simple and intuitive way to tackle this issue.

Witty Professor (WP): We have spent some time in this course talking about risk and return, but we never quite put them together. That's exactly what we'll do today, so let me start with an "easy" question: Say you decide to buy a few shares of Microsoft, what annual return would you require from those shares?

Insightful Student (IS): Wait a minute! We're just getting here! We're trying to warm up to a new topic and you hit us with that question? Are we even supposed to know that?

WP: Well, from the top of your head, what would you say?

IS: From the top of my head? I'd say I don't have the slightest idea!

WP: Well, you're certainly exaggerating. I'm sure that if I push you, you can do better than that, so I will. Let's say you take $100 out of your pocket and you put it safely in the bank for one year, what return would you expect to get?

IS: Whatever the bank gives me, I guess.

WP: Sure, with $100 you won't have any bargaining power, so you'll take whatever the bank offers you, or else you'll just keep the $100 in your pocket. But let's think a bit harder. Given that you'll put your money safely in the bank for one year, and that you'll bear no risk whatsoever, what is the minimum return you'd require?

IS: Well, given that I'll bear no risk, the least I'd require is not to lose purchasing power, so that I could buy in one year pretty much the same things I can buy today with $100.

WP: Or, in other words, no risk, no return, but no loss of purchasing power, either. Does that make sense?

IS: It does.

WP: OK, but my initial question was a bit more complicated: What if instead of putting your money in a riskless investment you buy shares of Microsoft?

IS: Well, first, if I'm buying shares of any company, my return is not guaranteed, so I do get to bear some risk.

Second, Microsoft strikes me as a particularly risky stock given that the company is in a volatile and rapidly changing sector.

WP: I knew you could do better than just saying that you don't have the slightest idea! Your intuition is correct. So, let's agree, first, that if you're buying stocks you'd require more return than you would if you were putting your money in a riskless investment. And let's also agree that you would not require the same return from all stocks; the riskier you perceive a company to be, the higher the return you would require. Do you agree?

IS: I do, on both counts.

WP: Great. So, believe it or not, we have already come a long way. We established that the required return on a stock has two components: a compensation for the expected loss of purchasing power and an extra compensation for bearing risk. We can even express this a bit more formally by writing

$$R_i = R_f + RP_i, \tag{1}$$

where R_i denotes the required return on stock i, R_f the risk-free rate, and RP_i the risk premium of stock i.

IS: That's easy enough, but how do we put numbers into those terms?

WP: Take it easy, don't get ahead of yourself. For now let's make sure we're clear about the fact that expression (1) says that the return we should require from the shares of a company has the two components we just mentioned: the risk-free rate (R_f), which is a compensation for the expected loss of purchasing power, and the risk premium (RP_i), which is a compensation for bearing the risk of investing in the company. Is that clear?

IS: It is. But why is it that only two of the three terms have a subscript *i*?

WP: Good question! The model we're discussing aims to calculate the required return on the shares of *any* company, which we simply call company *i*; that explains the R_i. And it also aims to link the return we should require from that company with the risk of holding shares of that company; that explains the RP_i. But notice that the return we require as a compensation for the expected loss of purchasing power is, and should be, the same for all our investments. Does that make sense?

IS: It does. What you're saying is that whether we invest in a riskless asset, or in the shares of a low-risk company, or in the shares of a high-risk company, we'll still require, at the very least, not to lose purchasing power. Therefore, although the risk premium is specific to the company in which we invest, the risk-free rate is the same regardless of the company in which we invest.

WP: Exactly. So, now let's take a look at what the CAPM, the Capital Asset Pricing Model, one of the models most widely used in finance, has to say about the estimation of the risk premium of stock *i*. This model simply says that we should estimate it as

$$RP_i = MRP \cdot \beta_i, \tag{2}$$

where *MPR* denotes the so-called market risk premium and β_i the beta of company *i*.

IS: Is that the same beta we discussed in one of our previous sessions?

WP: It is.

IS: And what about the market risk premium?

WP: Well, interestingly, the two terms in expression (2) have a very close parallel to the two statements that you agreed with a few minutes ago. You said that if you were to buy stocks you'd require more return than you would from a riskless investment. And you also said that the riskier you perceive a company to be, the higher the return you'd require. You still agree with those two statements?

IS: I sure do.

WP: Great, because the market risk premium is the additional compensation required by investors for investing in relatively riskier stocks as opposed to in relatively safer bonds. And now, let me ask you, can you guess why there is no subscript *i* in the market risk premium?

IS: I think so. Simply because we're talking about the comparison of two asset classes, stocks and bonds, and how much more return investors require to buy the riskier asset class.

WP: Exactly! And we'll talk about how to estimate that number in just a minute. But first, let me ask you, what about the second component of the risk premium?

IS: Well, as you said, that is the same beta we discussed earlier in the course, and therefore it measures the average return of a stock given a 1% fluctuation in the market. So stocks with betas larger than 1 magnify the market's fluctuations, and stocks with betas lower than 1 mitigate the market's fluctuations.

WP: Right again. And why the subscript *i*?

IS: Because now we're not talking about stocks versus bonds but about the specific company we're considering. So beta is related to the second statement I had agreed with before, that the riskier the company the higher the return I'd require.

WP: Exactly! Now can you summarize for me the intuition behind expression (2)?

IS: It's easy by now. The CAPM suggests that the risk premium of any stock has two components. One, the market risk premium, is the same for all stocks and measures the extra compensation required for investing in relatively riskier stocks as opposed to in relatively safer bonds. The other, beta, is specific to the company considered and measures the risk of investing in the shares of that company.

WP: Risk in general or something a bit more precise?

IS: It measures the *systematic* risk of investing in that company!

WP: Right! And, importantly, what is the CAPM implicitly assuming then?

IS: That investors hold diversified portfolios?

WP: Exactly! So, now we're ready to write the full expression of the CAPM, which in a perhaps not-too-technical but certainly accurate way is given by

$$R_i = R_f + MRP \cdot \beta_i, \qquad (3)$$

where all the terms are those we've been discussing.

IS: That looks pretty simple. I thought the CAPM would be more scary than that!

WP: It is pretty simple, though, as we'll soon see, the devil is in the details. But before we get there, tell me, in very easy terms that even your grandmother could understand, what is the intuition behind the way the CAPM suggests we should compute the required return on the shares of any company?

IS: The CAPM says that if we're going to invest in the shares of any company we should require return for two reasons. One, because we want to be compensated for our expected loss of purchasing power; that's the risk-free rate, and, as the name suggests, it is not related to risk. Two, because when we buy equity the return is not guaranteed and therefore we bear some risk; that's the risk premium and is made up of two components: one is the market risk premium, or the additional return required for investing in relatively riskier stocks as opposed to in relatively safer bonds, and the other is beta, the reaction of a stock to fluctuations in the market. How's that?

WP: Outstanding! But your phrasing invites a question. You talked about *required* returns; how are they different from *expected* returns?

IS: I think you got me there.

WP: Well, it's not that difficult. Although I do want to avoid getting into theoretical discussions here, let me just say that the CAPM is an equilibrium model, which means that what you require and what you expect *must* be the same.

IS: I'm not sure I follow you there.

WP: Well, if investors require 10% from a stock but they expect only 5%, they're obviously going to do something about it. They will sell the stock putting downward pressure on its price and increasing its expected return. The process will stop when the required and the expected return are the same. Can you make the other side of the argument?

IS: I think so. If investors require 5% from a stock but they expect 10% they will obviously buy, putting upward pressure on its price and lowering its expected return. And, again, the process will stop when the expected and the required return are the same. Is that correct?

WP: It is, so I hope it is clear now why some people talk about the CAPM as a model that yields *required* returns and others talk about it as a model that yields *expected* returns. In the equilibrium the CAPM considers both concepts are the same.

IS: I understand. But so far we haven't said anything about how to put specific numbers into expression (3).

WP: And we're getting to that right now. But remember we did talk about betas before, so putting numbers to betas should not be a problem, right?!

IS: Right. You suggested that betas are publicly available and rather easy to find, so instead of estimating them we should just stick to finding them in places like Yahoo Finance.

WP: Exactly. We may say a couple more things about them later, but let's first talk about the risk-free rate. We had agreed that it is the return required as a compensation for the expected loss of purchasing power, so how would you put a number to that?

IS: Well, as we discussed, that number should be pretty much in line with the expected rate of inflation, right?

WP: As a general argument that's correct. But are you suggesting that the average Joe in the street is knowledgeable about expected rates of inflation?

IS: No, that wouldn't make sense. I don't know. How do we come up with that number?

WP: Well, here's the thing with the CAPM. It is a very neat model, derived very elegantly from theory, and, as you can see from our discussion, very intuitive too. But, from a practical point of view, it is very vague in the sense that although it is clear what the three terms we need are, it is far from clear how we actually estimate them.

IS: Are you saying that the theory is clear but the actual application is not?

WP: Pretty much. Think about the risk-free rate. What magnitude would you use as a proxy for the expected loss of purchasing power, or, similarly, for the expected rate of inflation?

IS: I'm not sure, what would you use?

WP: Well, how about the yield on a government bond, which is risk-free if the bond is held until maturity?

IS: What do you mean by the yield?

WP: We'll talk about yields and bonds in more detail later in this course, but for the time being let's just say that the yield, or more precisely the yield to maturity, is the mean annual compound return you're going to get by buying the bond at the market price and holding it until maturity. You can easily find that number in the financial press and in financial web pages. So, do you think that yield would be a good proxy for the risk-free rate?

IS: Well, if we're talking about governments from developed countries, I do agree that they are risk-free, at least from a default perspective. But what maturity are you talking about? One year? Five? Ten? Thirty? Somewhere in between? Longer than 30 years?

WP: Good question. And here is precisely where it gets tricky. Theory won't help you, and in practice you'll find many and varied opinions. Some investors that deal with short-term projects would tend to favor short-term yields, and some investors that deal with long-term projects would tend to favor long-term yields. Then again, some would tend to favor using the same yield regardless of the length of the investments considered.

IS: So, what are we supposed to do?

WP: Basically two things. One, know that the issue is controversial and that there are many and varied opinions. Two, look for some consensus among practitioners.

IS: Is there anything close to consensus?

WP: Well, I'll go as far as saying that the 10-year yield is a very popular choice. It helps that it is the most widely followed yield, but it may also help that it looks like some sort of compromise between a short-term yield and a long-term yield.

IS: Should we then use the 10-year yield on government bonds as a proxy for the risk-free rate in the CAPM?

WP: Like I said, it's a popular choice, and if you use that you'll be in good company. But also know that some people may disagree, so be ready to hear some arguments against that choice.

IS: I think I can live with that. But what about the market risk premium? Is there also a controversy about how to calculate it?

WP: Yes, there is. Perhaps even more so than there is about the proper choice for the risk-free rate. Think about it. Remember that the market risk premium is the additional compensation required by investors for investing in relatively riskier stocks as opposed to in relatively safer bonds. How would you estimate that?

IS: No idea.

WP: Come on, try a bit harder.

IS: I guess I could look at the historical difference between the return of stocks and the return of bonds and assume that in the future the difference will be pretty much as it's been in the past.

WP: Very good! Estimating the risk premium based on historical data, though by no means the only way of doing it, is a very popular choice. But your answer is still quite vague, isn't it? What do you mean by the return of stocks? The return of the Dow? Of the S&P? Of an even more comprehensive index? And what about the return of bonds? Is that the return of one-year bonds? Five-year bonds? Ten? Thirty? Corporate bonds? Government bonds?

IS: Lots of questions!

WP: And I'm not done! What do you mean by historical? The past 30 years? The past 60? The past 100? And what kind of historical average are you going to take, arithmetic or geometric?

IS: I think I speak for all my classmates if I say I'm overwhelmed!

WP: Well, don't feel too bad. I'm throwing all this at you because I want to make sure you understand that estimating the market risk premium opens a lot of questions, and, like putting a number to the risk-free rate, there is a wide variety of more or less reasonable answers.

IS: So, what are we supposed to do?

WP: Well, let me first remind you once again that the issue is controversial and that there are many answers to your question. And, second, let me also remind you that this course is very practical and that whenever we can take a shortcut we do, so take a look at Exhibit 5.1, which shows the market risk premium for several countries over the 1900–2000 period.

IS: And what are we supposed to do with this exhibit?

WP: Well, don't you think it gives you a good idea about the historical number you proposed to estimate? The figures in Exhibit 5.1 give you a cross-country view and a long-term perspective. Also, they are estimated with respect to both bills and bonds and based on both arithmetic and geometric averages. And perhaps I should add that they come from the most comprehensive database of long-term data for international markets.

Exhibit 5.1

Country	With respect to bills		With respect to bonds	
	Geometric (%)	Arithmetic (%)	Geometric (%)	Arithmetic (%)
Australia	7.1	8.5	6.3	8.0
Belgium	2.9	5.1	2.9	4.8
Canada	4.6	5.9	4.5	6.0
Denmark	1.8	3.4	2.0	3.3
France	7.4	9.8	4.9	7.0
Germany	4.9	10.3	6.7	9.9
Ireland	3.5	5.4	3.2	4.6
Italy	7.0	11.0	5.0	8.4
Japan	6.7	9.9	6.2	10.3
Netherlands	5.1	7.1	4.7	6.7
South Africa	6.0	8.1	5.4	7.1
Spain	3.2	5.3	2.3	4.2
Sweden	5.5	7.7	5.2	7.4
Switzerland	4.3	6.1	2.7	4.2
UK	4.8	6.5	4.4	5.6
USA	5.8	7.7	5.0	7.0
World	4.9	6.2	4.6	5.6

Source: Adapted from Elroy Dimson, Paul Marsh, and Mike Staunton, *Triumph of the Optimists: 101 Years of Global Investment Returns*, Princeton, NJ: Princeton University Press, 2002.

IS: So you're saying that if we need to use a market risk premium we can basically pick a number from the table, right?

WP: Right. The table will not solve all your problems, but it's a good starting point. You'll still have to decide whether you will use a number with respect to bills or bonds or based on arithmetic or geometric averages.

IS: So, what should we do?

WP: Well, when estimating the market risk premium in the USA, the interval between 5% and 6% seems to be a rather popular choice, and, as you can see in Exhibit 5.1, that closely matches the market risk premium based on geometric averages. If you choose a number in this interval, you may find some people that disagree with your choice, and perhaps rightly so, but again you will be in good company.

IS: So, you're saying that the widely used interval between 5% and 6% can be justified by historical data?

WP: Exactly. But, again, make sure you keep in mind that there is a wide variety of ways of estimating the market risk premium, and empirically that yields a wide range of possible estimates. So, yet again, be ready to hear some arguments against that choice.

IS: And what about for other countries?

WP: Well, as you can see in Exhibit 5.1, the numbers differ quite a bit across countries. That means that each country has its own market risk premium, just as much as each country has its own risk-free rate.

IS: I think I get it. And what about beta?

WP: I think it's best if, as we discussed before, you stick to finding betas in sites like Yahoo Finance rather than calculating them. But if you want to know just a bit more, I'll go as far as saying that a popular way to estimate betas is based on five years of monthly data.

IS: Why five years?

WP: Yet again it's another compromise, in this case between not going too many years back so that we may end up using data on a company very different from the one we observe today; and not going too few years back so that we may end up considering only a very good or very bad short-term situation.

IS: And why monthly data?

WP: Monthly data is, from a statistical point of view, much better behaved than weekly or daily data, but, as I asked you a few times before, you don't want me to get into statistical discussions, do you?

IS: No, I guess we don't. But can you give us an example of how to calculate a required return on equity based on the CAPM?

WP: Sure, I was just getting to that. And since my initial question to you was about Microsoft, let's close this discussion with that company. So here we go. Halfway into 2008, the yield on 10-year US Treasury notes was, roughly, 3.9%. Let's use 5.5% as the market risk premium, which is the midpoint of the popular 5–6% interval. Finally, according to Yahoo Finance, the beta of Microsoft is 1.3. Then, the required return on Microsoft stock according to the CAPM is

$$R_{Microsoft} = 3.9\% + (5.5\%)(1.3) = 11.1\%.$$

IS: That's pretty easy!

WP: It is, but it's important that you don't forget that we're making very specific choices for the risk-free rate, the market risk premium, and beta; and that many people could reasonably question our choices. And, of course, different choices would yield a different number. So, like just about everything else in finance, you have to have good reasons for your choices so you can defend them in a reasonable way.

IS: Wrap-up time?

WP: I thought you'd never ask! The CAPM is the model most widely used to estimate the required return of stocks and is supported by an elegant theory and a clear intuition. The model argues that investors require a return for their expected loss of purchasing power and an additional return for bearing risk. This second component has two parts: a compensation required for investing in relatively riskier stocks as opposed to in relatively safer bonds and an adjustment for the average reaction of a stock to fluctuations in the market. In practice, the three components of the model, the risk-free rate, the market risk premium, and beta, can be estimated in a variety of ways. Some ways are more popular than others but the model's implementation leaves ample room for reasonable disagreement. Coffee time now?

Tool 6
Downside Risk

This chapter discusses a view of risk that, unlike the standard deviation and beta, focuses on the downside faced by investors. Of the several measures that attempt to capture this downside, the focus here is on the semi-deviation, an increasingly popular magnitude that measures volatility below any chosen benchmark.

Witty Professor (WP): Today we'll talk about risk, again, but from a different point of view to that which we have discussed before. So how about if we start by summarizing, very briefly, the risk measures we've discussed so far?

Insightful Student (IS): So far we've discussed two measures of risk: the standard deviation and beta. When an asset is considered in isolation, we bear its total risk, which we can quantify with the standard deviation of its returns. When an asset is part of a diversified portfolio, its unsystematic risk gets diversified away, and we bear only its systematic, nondiversifiable risk, which we can quantify with its beta. How's that?

WP: That's very good. Now let me ask you: Can you see any problems with the standard deviation as a measure of risk?

IS: No, are there any?

WP: Think a bit harder!

IS: Well, one thing that caught my attention when we discussed the standard deviation a couple of sessions ago is that it seems to treat a return x% below and above the mean in the same way.

WP: What do you mean by that?

IS: I mean that if a return is, say, 5% above or below the mean, it would contribute in the same magnitude to the final figure for the standard deviation.

WP: Why?

IS: Well, simply because when we calculate the standard deviation we square the differences between each return and the mean return, and once you do that you end up with a positive number regardless of whether the return was above or below the mean.

WP: Very good. Now, tell me, is it the same for you to have one of your stocks jumping 5% above or below its mean return?

IS: Of course not! Jumps above the mean make me happy, jumps below it make me unhappy!

WP: In other words, you feel differently about returns above and below the mean, right?

IS: I sure do!

WP: But the standard deviation as a measure of risk, as you yourself said, does not make any distinction between x% jumps above and below the mean. Do you think that's plausible?

IS: No, it's not. I guess that a plausible measure of risk should consider only returns below the mean, not above it.

WP: But why should we focus on departures with respect to the mean? Why not with respect to the risk-free rate? Or the rate of inflation? Or 0? Or any other benchmark that may be interesting to an investor?

IS: You're right, there's no special reason for restricting the benchmark to the mean.

WP: Well, it turns out that a magnitude that measures volatility below any chosen benchmark exists, and we'll discuss it today. But before we do, let me stress with an example one of the main weakness of the standard deviation as a measure of risk. Take a look at Exhibit 6.1, which in its second column shows the annual returns (R) of Oracle between 1998 and 2007.

IS: Wow! That was quite a rocky ride for Oracle's shareholders!

WP: It was. And the volatility of 91.2% that you can see in the exhibit seems to confirm that, right?

IS: Right.

WP: Now, you already know how to calculate a stand-ard deviation, but let's take the long road here. The

Exhibit 6.1

Year	R (%)	R − AM (%)	(R − AM)²	Min(R − AM, 0) (%)	{Min(R − AM, 0)}²
1998	93.3	53.3	0.2845	0.0	0.0000
1999	289.6	249.6	6.2320	0.0	0.0000
2000	3.7	−36.3	0.1315	−36.3	0.1315
2001	−52.5	−92.5	0.8549	−92.5	0.8549
2002	−21.8	−61.8	0.3814	−61.8	0.3814
2003	22.5	−17.5	0.0305	−17.5	0.0305
2004	3.7	−36.3	0.1315	−36.3	0.1315
2005	−11.0	−51.0	0.2597	−51.0	0.2597
2006	40.4	0.4	0.0000	0.0	0.0000
2007	31.7	−8.3	0.0068	−8.3	0.0068
Average	40.0	−	0.8313	−	0.1796
Square root (%)	−	−	91.2	−	42.4

third column of the exhibit shows each annual return minus Oracle's arithmetic mean return *(AM)* of 40%, and the fourth column shows the square of the numbers in the third column. Now let me ask you, if we take the average of the numbers in the fourth column, what do we get?

IS: That's easy: the variance of Oracle's returns. By definition, the variance is the average quadratic deviation with respect to the mean. And, as we discussed a couple of sessions ago, that's a number expressed in "percent square," whatever that means, and without much intuition.

WP: Very good. And if we want the standard deviation of Oracle's returns?

IS: Then we simply take the square root of the variance, and the resulting number will be expressed in percent.

So, if we take the square root of 0.8313 we get that 91.2% we can see in the last row of the exhibit.

WP: Great. Now take a good look at the numbers in the fourth column and tell me, of all the numbers you see there, which is the one that contributes the most to the final figure we calculate for the standard deviation.

IS: That's obvious: it's the 6.2320 that corresponds to the year 1999.

WP: Correct. Now, tell me, what return did Oracle's shareholders get that year?

IS: A spectacular 289.6%!

WP: Can you see the irony of that then?

IS: I sure can! In 1999, Oracle's shareholders got a spectacular return of almost 300%, which should have made them laugh all the way to the bank. But at the same time that return increased the standard deviation, a measure of risk, dramatically. So the standard deviation suggests that returns so high above the mean are "bad" because they increase risk! It's almost funny when you think of it.

WP: Well, that's precisely the main problem of the standard deviation as a measure of risk. Wouldn't you prefer a measure of risk that counts as "bad" only the returns that are *below* the mean? Or, more generally, wouldn't you prefer a measure of risk that counts as "bad" only the returns *below any benchmark of your choice*?

IS: I sure would!

WP: Well, again, there is such a risk measure, and we'll discuss it right now. And, just for the moment, let's stick with the mean return as the benchmark. Take a look at the fifth column of Exhibit 6.1, which shows what we can call "conditional returns." And we can call them that because we calculate them by asking an "if... then ..." question. Can you guess what the question or condition is?

IS: I think so. The header of the column suggests that we take the minimum of the annual return minus the mean return or 0. So, if in any given year the return is lower than the mean return, the "conditional return" is the return for that year minus the mean return; if, on the other hand, the return is higher than the mean return, then the "conditional return" is 0. For example, in 1998, the 93.3% return is higher than the mean return of 40%, so the "conditional return" is 0%; but in 2000, the 3.7% return was lower than the mean return of 40%, so the "conditional return" was 3.7% – 40.0% = –36.3%. Is that correct?

WP: It is. And, as you can see in that fifth column, we end up with "conditional returns" that are either negative, when annual returns are lower than the mean return; or 0, when annual returns are higher than the mean return.

IS: Which explains why the figures in the last column, which are just the square of those in the fifth column, show a 0 in the years when returns are higher than the mean and a positive number in the years when returns are lower than the mean, right?

WP: Exactly! Now, if we take the average of all those numbers in the last column, we obtain what is called the semivariance of returns with respect to the mean. But, as usual, we're not going to focus on a number expressed in "percent squared" but on something more intuitive. So, if we take the square root of the semivariance, we obtain the semideviation, which, in this case is, more precisely, the *semideviation with respect to the mean*, a magnitude expressed in percent.

IS: So, 0.1796 is the semivariance with respect to the mean, and the square root of that number, 42.4%, is the semideviation with respect to the mean, right?

WP: Correct. And now let's think about this magnitude. What do you think it measures?

IS: Well, given our discussion so far, and a few hints you've been dropping here and there, I'd say that this semideviation measures *volatility below the mean return of 40%*.

WP: Exactly. That's the correct and more straightforward interpretation of this magnitude. Now take another good look at the numbers we used to calculate this semideviation, those in the last column of Exhibit 6.1. Compare them to those we used to calculate the standard deviation, those in the fourth column of the exhibit. Is there anything that catches your attention?

IS: Yes, two things, actually. And let me start by saying that the only 0.0000 in the fourth column must obviously be a very small but positive number because the 40.4% return for 2006 is just a tiny bit higher than the

40.0% mean return. Having said that, I notice that in the last column some of the numbers are positive and some are 0, unlike the numbers in the fourth column, which are all positive. In other words, *all* returns contribute to the final figure for the standard deviation (unless they're equal to the mean return), but only the returns that are *below* the mean return contribute to the final figure for the semideviation.

WP: Exactly. And the other thing that caught your attention?

IS: Well, as we discussed before, the return that contributes the most to the final figure for the standard deviation is that 289.6% for the year 1999, which actually should have made shareholders very happy. However, we can see in the last column that for the year 1999 we have a 0, which means that such a great return does not count against Oracle by increasing the semideviation. It makes perfect sense!

WP: It does, and that is, precisely, one of the most interesting characteristics of the semideviation as a measure of risk: Returns above the benchmark, in this case the mean return, do not increase the semideviation; only returns below the benchmark do.

IS: That, of course, makes sense. But you suggested before that there's no reason why the mean return should necessarily be the benchmark, right?

WP: That's right. If you think about it, the mean return seems to be a rather uninteresting benchmark, doesn't it? Most investors would find other benchmarks more relevant. As we mentioned before, for some investors the benchmark could be the risk-free rate, for others the rate of inflation, for others 0, for others a target return they'd like to obtain – you name it.

IS: Are you suggesting that the semideviation can handle all those different benchmarks?

WP: Yes, it can, and very easily. Just notice that the "conditional returns" in Exhibit 6.1 were based on whether each annual return was higher or lower than the mean return. But, of course, we could just as easily calculate "conditional returns" based on whether each annual return is higher or lower than any benchmark of our choice.

IS: I think I can see that, but still can you give us an example?

WP: Sure, take a look at Exhibit 6.2. The last three columns show the square of "conditional returns" with respect to three benchmarks: the mean return of 40% (which is the one we've been discussing), a risk-free rate (R_f) of 5% and 0%.

IS: Let me see if I understand. Each number in the last three columns is the square of a "conditional return" defined as the minimum of an annual return minus the chosen benchmark or 0. That means that for 1998, because the 93.3% return for that year is higher than the mean return of 40%, a risk-free rate of 5%, and 0%, in the last three columns we have a 0; and for 2001,

Exhibit 6.2

Year	R (%)	$\{Min(R - AM, 0)\}^2$	$\{Min(R - R_f, 0)\}^2$	$\{Min(R - 0, 0)\}^2$
1998	93.3	0.0000	0.0000	0.0000
1999	289.6	0.0000	0.0000	0.0000
2000	3.7	0.1315	0.0002	0.0000
2001	−52.5	0.8549	0.3306	0.2756
2002	−21.8	0.3814	0.0718	0.0475
2003	22.5	0.0305	0.0000	0.0000
2004	3.7	0.1315	0.0002	0.0000
2005	−11.0	0.2597	0.0256	0.0121
2006	40.4	0.0000	0.0000	0.0000
2007	31.7	0.0068	0.0000	0.0000
Average	40.0	0.1796	0.0428	0.0335
Square Root (%)	–	42.4	20.7	18.3

because the −52.5% return for that year is lower than the mean return of 40%, a risk-free rate of 5%, and 0%, we have $(-52.5\% - 40.0\%)^2 = 0.8549$, $(-52.5\% - 5.0\%)^2 = 0.3306$, and $(-52.5\% - 0\%)^2 = 0.2756$. Is that correct?

WP: Perfectly correct. So the last three columns of Exhibit 6.2 show the square of "conditional returns" with respect to three different benchmarks, the mean return of 40%, a risk-free rate of 5%, and 0%; the next-to-last row shows the semivariances with respect to these three benchmarks (0.1796, 0.0428, and 0.0335); and the last row shows the semideviations with respect to the same benchmarks (42.4%, 20.7%, and 18.3%).

IS: And how should we interpret these semideviations?

WP: As we suggested before, basically as volatility *below* the three chosen benchmarks. Note that because 0% is lower than a risk-free rate of 5%, which in turn is lower than the mean return of 40%, then we would expect to find, and do find, less volatility below 5% than below 40%, and less volatility below 0% than below 5%.

IS: I see. But what about when we compare semideviations across assets? If we use the mean return as the benchmark, then we'd be comparing volatility below different numbers. Does that make sense?

WP: Excellent point! In fact, the best way to use semideviations when comparing risk across different assets is to use the same benchmark for all assets.

IS: That makes sense. Can you give us an example?

WP: Sure. Take a look at Exhibit 6.3, which shows the arithmetic mean return (*AM*) and volatility (*SD*) of Oracle and Microsoft, as well as the semideviation with respect to the mean return (SSD_{AM}), with respect to a risk-free rate of 5% (SSD_{Rf}), and with respect to 0% (SSD_0). And before we get to the semideviations, please do notice that, if we thought of the standard deviation as the proper measure of risk, then we should conclude that Oracle is far riskier than Microsoft, right?

IS: Well, given volatilities of 91.2% for Oracle and 46.6% for Microsoft, yes, we should conclude that Oracle is far riskier than Microsoft.

Exhibit 6.3

Company	*AM* (%)	*SD* (%)	SSD_{AM} (%)	SSD_{Rf} (%)	SSD_0 (%)
Oracle	40.0	91.2	42.4	20.7	18.3
Microsoft	20.2	46.6	30.8	23.2	21.1

WP: OK, hold on to that conclusion, and let's consider now the semideviations with respect to each stock's mean return. In this case, as the exhibit shows, we get 42.4% for Oracle and 30.8% for Microsoft, suggesting again that Oracle is riskier than Microsoft, right?

IS: Right, but here's where the point I made before applies. The mean return of Oracle, 40%, is much higher than that of Microsoft, 20.2%, so we're measuring volatility below two very different benchmarks.

WP: Exactly. And what happens when we assess the relative risk of Oracle and Microsoft by using the semideviation with respect to the same benchmark for both stocks, such as a risk-free rate of 5% or 0%?

IS: Well, if the benchmark is a risk-free rate of 5%, then Oracle's semideviation of 20.7% is lower than Microsoft's 23.2%; and if the benchmark is 0%, then Oracle's semideviation of 18.3% is lower than Microsoft's 21.1%. So, in both cases we conclude that Oracle is *less* risky than Microsoft. That's interesting! It's the opposite conclusion we reached by assessing the relative risk of the two stocks with the standard deviation!

WP: Exactly. And of course it doesn't always have to be the case, but as this example shows, it's perfectly possible that if you assess the risk of two assets by using the standard deviation, you reach a different conclusion than you would if you used the semideviation.

IS: Which implies that one would have to have good reasons to choose one measure of risk over the other, right? After all, if the choice of one magnitude or the other may lead us to opposite conclusions, we'd better make a good choice!

WP: Right again. And here's where the matter of plausibility we discussed before comes in: which of the two, the standard deviation or the semideviation, is more plausible is critical. In any case, when you compare the risk of different assets, whether you do it with the standard deviation, or the semideviation, or any other risk measure, you always have to keep in mind what you're really assessing. Or, put differently, you always have to keep in mind how you're defining risk. That's very important.

IS: I understand, but I do have a couple of doubts. First, it seems obvious that, for any given asset, if two investors have different benchmarks, then they will come up with different semideviations, right? But that doesn't happen with the standard deviation; different investors considering the same asset will come up with exactly the same number. Isn't that "objectivity," for lack of a better term, a strength of the standard deviation and a weakness of the semideviation?

WP: That's a very good question. Some people argue just that, and there is some plausibility in the argument. But, on the other hand, isn't it the case that different investors, for perfectly good reasons, may have different benchmarks, and, as a result, each of them will care about volatility below their chosen benchmark? Isn't there some plausibility in that argument too?

IS: Yes, there is. My other doubt is that we usually think of volatility as "bad," but this downside risk framework seems to suggest that not all volatility is "bad"; volatility below the benchmark increases the semideviation and is undesirable, but volatility above the benchmark does not increase the semideviation and may even be desirable. Am I interpreting that correctly?

WP: You are. In fact, in a downside risk framework, volatility is usually characterized as "good" or "bad" depending on whether it is above or below the chosen benchmark. And, as much as it should be clear by now why volatility below the benchmark is undesirable, it should also be clear why volatility above the benchmark is desirable. After all, don't all investors like returns like that 289.6% that Oracle delivered in 1999?!

IS: Yes, of course! Well, I think I'm sold on the semideviation. I do find it a plausible measure of risk, even more so than the standard deviation. So, are you going to give us the expression to calculate it?

WP: No need to. The expression is somewhat intimidating, and at the end of the day it should be clear from our previous discussion how to calculate it. Actually, you tell me, how would you do it?

IS: Well, first I'd input the returns of the relevant asset along a column of a spreadsheet; then, in the next column, I'd calculate the "conditional returns" with respect to the chosen benchmark; then, in the next column, I'd square those "conditional returns"; then, in any empty cell I'd take the average of the squared "conditional returns," which would give me the semi-variance; and then in some other empty cell I'd take the square root of the semivariance, finally obtaining the semideviation. That's pretty much what we did in Exhibit 6.1. Correct?

WP: Perfectly correct!

IS: And if we wanted to calculate the semideviation in just one cell, as we do with the standard deviation?

WP: Then you're going to have to wait until our optional session on some useful Excel commands after we finish the ten core sessions of this course. And now, if there are no more questions or comments, wrap-up time!

IS: No more questions, no more comments!

WP: Well, here we go then. The standard deviation is one of the most widely used measures of risk, but it is also somewhat implausible. First, it uses the arithmetic mean as a benchmark; investors, however, usually have other benchmarks in mind. Second, and more importantly, it gives the same weight to $x\%$ returns above and below the mean; investors, obviously, do not feel the same way about these returns. The semideviation, a measure of downside risk, deals with both problems neatly: It enables investors to set any benchmark of their choice, and accounts only for volatility below the chosen benchmark. And that, my dear insightful student, sounds like a plausible measure of risk, doesn't it? Which brings me to the fact that this professor, like Elvis, has just left the building!

Tool 7
Risk-Adjusted Returns

This chapter discusses how to properly evaluate performance by taking into account not just return, as most commercial rankings do, but also risk. And because risk can
be defined in more than one way, there is more than
one measure of risk-adjusted returns. We will discuss five
of them, some differing in the way they define risk and
others in the way they incorporate it into a risk-adjusted
measure.

Witty Professor (WP): In this course we have talked
about returns, we have talked about risk, and we have
related them to one another through the CAPM. Today,
we'll talk about returns and risk, and we'll put them
together again.

Insightful Student (IS): Well, if we're going to just repeat
what we've done before I guess I'll just sit back and
relax!

WP: Well, you'd better sit right on the edge of that
chair because all the material to be discussed is new.

Yes, we'll talk about risk and return again, and, yes, we'll put them together again, but the focus will be different. First, we'll put them together in such a way as to measure the returns we get relative to the risk we bear; second, we'll use those measures of risk-adjusted returns to properly rank the performance of assets.

IS: Oh, that sounds interesting. Actually, just last week a well-known financial newspaper published a ranking of mutual funds.

WP: Great, let's talk about that. How were the funds ranked?

IS: They were split into several categories, like small stocks, value stocks, emerging markets stocks, and so forth, and the ranking for each category was based on the funds'return for the previous three months.

WP: And what did you think when you found out who were the best and worst performers?

IS: Well, at the beginning I thought the information was very useful, and that if I had any money to invest I'd distribute it among the top performers of some categories.

WP: And then you had second thoughts?

IS: Yes, because it occurred to me that given that the ranking was based on the returns for the past three months, some fund managers may have just been lucky and some others just unlucky.

WP: What do you mean by lucky or unlucky? Fund managers are not supposed to rely on luck to do their jobs, are they?

IS: No, but it seems to me that in any given quarter some of the managers' stock picks may have performed surprisingly well or poorly, and that such unexpected performance, rather than their knowledge, may have pushed them to the top or the bottom of the ranking. After all, although I know nothing about horse racing, maybe one day I might bet and win, which of course shouldn't lead you to believe that I know anything about horses. You can only evaluate my ability to pick winning horses after you observe many, not just one, of my choices.

WP: Good thinking! Fund managers, just like all of us, can get lucky or unlucky over a short period of time, and we should not think of them highly or poorly just because of that. Unfortunately, there are lots of bad investors out there, and short-term returns do seem to be associated with flows of money into and out of funds.

IS: What do you mean?

WP: That rankings like the one you saw, based on returns for the past quarter or year, play a role in determining where some investors put their money. These investors seem to think that good and bad performers over the past quarter or year will also be good and bad performers over the next several years. Of course, nothing's farther from the truth.

IS: So you're saying that when we evaluate fund managers we should do it on the basis of their long-term returns rather than on the basis of their returns last quarter or last year, right?

WP: Not quite. Evaluating their returns over the long term is better than doing it over the short term. But assessing their returns is not enough; we also need to bring risk into the picture. Actually, you should be able to see why. Can you?

IS: Well, since risk and return are positively related, in the long term we should be able to get higher returns if we're willing to be exposed to more risk, right?

WP: Right. So?

IS: Well, I can always load my portfolio with risky stocks and expect a high long-term return, but that high return is not a free lunch; it's just the result of my high exposure to risk. In other words, if all you give me as a fund manager is high returns that follow exclusively from a high exposure to risk, you're not really giving me anything I can't pretty much replicate. I wouldn't put you at the top of my ranking because of that!

WP: Good thinking again! That's exactly the heart of our discussion today. We'll talk about how to rank not only fund managers but also assets in general by taking into account *both* the return they deliver *and* the risk they expose investors to.

IS: All the while trying to isolate risk and return from the impact of luck by considering a long period of time, right?

WP: That's right. We'll take out the impact of luck by evaluating long-term as opposed to short-term returns. And we'll account for the impact of risk on returns by calculating risk-adjusted returns, which is what we'll do in a minute. At the end of the day, a proper evaluation of fund managers, or assets in general, should be made on the basis of long-term, risk-adjusted returns. And, of course, the higher these are, the better.

IS: So, those assets or managers at the top of a ranking based on long-term, risk-adjusted returns are, all relevant things considered, the best ones, those we want to invest in.

WP: As long as you remember that good past performance does not *guarantee* good future performance, yes. But it's probably better to think that solid past performers are only *likely* to be solid future performers.

IS: Roger that. Please continue.

WP: Well, I think it's useful to start with an example, so take a look at Exhibit 7.1, which shows some summary statistics for the MSCI indices of four emerging equity

Exhibit 7.1

Market	AM (%)	SD (%)	Beta	SSD_{Rf} (%)
Chile	16.1	23.7	1.1	16.5
Israel	16.0	25.7	1.0	17.5
Poland	18.4	34.4	1.5	22.6
South Africa	18.1	28.8	1.3	20.2
World	9.5	14.3	1.0	10.3

Note: Semideviations based on a risk-free rate of 4%.

markets – Chile, Israel, Poland, and South Africa – as well as for the world market, over the 1998–2007 period. As you can see, based on their arithmetic mean annual returns (*AM*), the Polish market outperformed all the other markets considered.

IS: Are those returns in dollars or in the local currency of each country?

WP: Good question. All returns are in dollars and account for both capital gains and dividends. Also, the beta of each market is calculated with respect to the world market. And since all these figures are based on a ten-year period, let's rather safely assume that luck will not play a role in our evaluation. In other words, our rankings will not be based on just a very good or very bad quarter or year for these markets but on a much longer history.

IS: OK, so, luck not being an issue, the exhibit shows that Poland was the best performing market, closely followed by South Africa, with Chile and Israel somewhat behind.

WP: If we focus just on returns, that's correct. But, as you mentioned before, risk also needs to be taken into account. So, the problem with claiming that Poland was the best performing market of those considered in the exhibit, which is what most commercial rankings would do, is that it was also the riskiest market; and that is the case regardless of whether we assess risk with the standard deviation (*SD*), beta, or the semideviation with respect to a risk-free rate (SSD_{Rf}).

IS: So you're saying that we should not rush to conclude that Poland was the best performing market. You do acknowledge that it was the one that delivered the highest returns, but you're calling our attention to the fact that it was also the riskiest market. That much is clear. What is not clear, at least to me, is how we can put risk and return together in a number to determine which one was the best performing market.

WP: And we're going to talk about that right now. But before we start with definitions, let me clarify, first, that when we talk about the "return" of an asset, we'll really be talking about the asset's *mean* return. Second, that this *arithmetic* mean return has been calculated over a "long" period of time, which is ten years (1998–2007) in our case. And third, that by "long" we simply mean long enough so that we're fairly sure that luck has played little or no role. OK?

IS: OK. As we said before, we need to evaluate assets on the basis of their long-term, risk-adjusted returns, and for that we need to consider their long-term track record.

WP: Exactly. So here we go. Let's start with one of the most widely-used measures of risk-adjusted returns, the so-called *Jensen's alpha*, or simply *alpha* (α_i) which is defined as

$$\alpha_i = R_i - (R_f + MRP \cdot \beta_i) , \tag{1}$$

where R_i and β_i denote the return and beta of asset i, and R_f and MRP the risk-free rate and the market risk premium. So, right off the bat, let me ask you, what is the term in parentheses?

IS: That seems to be the expression of the CAPM, which means that what we have in parentheses is the required or expected return of asset *i*, right?

WP: Correct. And that means that we're considering what kind of risk?

IS: Well, if we measure risk with beta, then we're considering systematic risk.

WP: And what is the implicit assumption behind this alpha, then?

IS: That investors are diversified and for that reason they only bear the systematic risk of the asset considered, right?

WP: Right again. And now, tell me, can you see what the intuition behind this alpha is?

IS: I think so. We start with the mean return actually delivered by the asset, and we subtract from it its required or expected return. If the asset delivered a higher return than we required, then alpha is positive; in the opposite case, alpha is negative.

WP: Which means?

IS: Which means that assets with a positive alpha are "good" because they delivered a higher return than we required, and assets with a negative alpha are "bad" because they delivered a lower return than we required.

WP: Or, in other words, assets with a positive alpha performed above our expectations, and those with negative alpha performed below our expectations. And, of course, the higher the alpha, the more attractive the asset. Now, take a look at the second column of Exhibit 7.2, which shows the alphas of the emerging markets we've been considering, all calculated for a risk-free rate of 4% and a world market risk premium of 5.5%. I assume you can reproduce how these alphas were calculated, right?

IS: Well, let's take Chile. Given that, as shown in Exhibit 7.1, its mean return has been 16.1% and its beta 1.1, then its alpha must have been calculated as $0.161 - (0.04 + 0.055 \cdot 1.1) = 6.1\%$.

WP: Perfect. The other alphas were calculated in a similar way. Now take another look at the second column of Exhibit 7.2, compare it to the second column of Exhibit 7.1, and tell me if there's anything that catches your attention.

IS: Yes! Poland, the best-performing market in terms of returns, is outperformed by South Africa and Israel in

Exhibit 7.2

Market	Alpha (%)	Treynor	Sharpe	RAP (%)	Sortino
Chile	6.1	0.110	0.511	11.3	0.733
Israel	6.5	0.120	0.467	10.7	0.686
Poland	6.2	0.096	0.419	10.0	0.637
South Africa	7.0	0.108	0.490	11.0	0.698
World	0.0	0.055	0.385	9.5	0.534

Note: All figures based on a risk-free rate of 4% and a (world) market risk premium of 5.5%.

terms of risk-adjusted returns. And Israel, the worst-performing market in terms of returns, is the second best in terms of risk-adjusted returns. So it does make a difference whether we evaluate and rank assets in terms of returns or risk-adjusted returns!

WP: It does. And, as we'll see in a minute, how we define risk and risk-adjusted returns also makes a difference. But before we consider another magnitude, let me make three points on this alpha. First, note that although the alphas of the four emerging markets on Exhibit 7.2 are all positive, it is perfectly possible to find negative alphas. Taiwan, for example, an emerging market not shown in our exhibits, had over the 1998–2007 period an alpha of –3.8%.

IS: And that means that it delivered mean annual returns almost 4% below its required or expected return, right?

WP: Exactly, which brings me to my second point: Alpha is a very intuitive magnitude that shows by how many percentage points we exceed or fall short from our required return. The 7% alpha for South Africa simply indicates that this market delivered a mean annual return 7% higher than we required or expected; and the –3.8% alpha for Taiwan has exactly the interpretation you just gave to it.

IS: And the third point?

WP: The third point is a shortcoming of alpha. Can you see what it might be?

IS: Not really, it looks quite plausible to me.

WP: Well, suppose you have two assets that over the past ten years had delivered an alpha of 2%. Measured by alpha, these two assets are equally attractive because they delivered the same risk-adjusted return, right?

IS: Right.

WP: Well, suppose that one asset has a much higher beta, and therefore a much higher required return, than the other. Let's say that the required return on the first asset is 4% and that on the second is 20%. Knowing this, would you still consider both assets equally attractive?

IS: No, not really. Both delivered a return 2% above our required return, but in the first case 2% is 50% (= 2%/4%) above our expectation, and in the second case 2% is only 10% (= 2%/20%) above our expectation. In other words, both assets delivered the same *absolute* outperformance but the first asset delivered a better *relative* outperformance.

WP: Exactly! So, alphas are very widely used, and for very good reasons, but just keep in mind this shortcoming when you use them. In fact, our next measure of risk-adjusted returns overcomes this limitation of alpha. The **Treynor ratio (T_i)** is defined as

$$T_i = (R_i - R_f)/\beta_i , \qquad (2)$$

where the numerator, $R_i - R_f$, is often referred to as excess returns, and risk is again measured by beta. The third column of Exhibit 7.2 shows the Treynor ratios for the emerging markets we're considering, and I assume you can reproduce how these magnitudes were calculated, right?

IS: It should be easy. Let's take Chile again; its Treynor ratio must have been calculated as $(0.161 - 0.04)/1.1 = 0.110$. But I do have a question. If the Treynor ratio measures risk with beta, what is its contribution beyond what we can gather from alpha, which also measures risk with beta?

WP: The contribution is basically to take care of the shortcoming of alpha we just discussed. Note that the Treynor ratio measures excess returns *per unit of (beta) risk*, which means that we're measuring absolute returns *relative to* the beta risk we bear. For this reason, a ranking of assets on the basis of the Treynor ratio is methodologically superior to one on the basis of alpha. Having said that, the Treynor ratio does have a shortcoming of its own; can you see what it might be?

IS: Well, alpha is measured in percent so it's very intuitive, but it seems to me that this Treynor ratio is a magnitude without much intuition. Anybody can understand that an asset outperformed its expected return by, say, 2%, but there does not seem to be much intuition behind a Treynor ratio of, say, 0.354.

WP: Exactly. And precisely for that reason, Treynor ratios are typically not used to assess the risk-adjusted performance of an individual asset but rather the *relative* risk-adjusted performance of several assets. In other words, they are largely used to simply rank assets.

IS: And I notice from the third column of Exhibit 7.2 that although alpha and the Treynor ratio both use beta as the measure of risk, a ranking of assets by these two magnitudes may differ from each other, right?

WP: Exactly. As you can see in the exhibit, Israel is now the best performing market, and Poland, the star performer in terms of returns, the worst performing market. None of the numbers you see in that third column taken in isolation is very intuitive, but when you put them all together, they appropriately rank assets by their risk-adjusted performance.

IS: And you said before that a ranking by the Treynor ratio is better than a ranking by alpha, right?

WP: Yes, the Treynor ratio overcomes the shortcoming of alpha and provides a more appropriate ranking of risk-adjusted performance. Having said that, in practice you will find that alphas, perhaps because they are much easier to communicate and discuss, are far more widely used than Treynor ratios.

IS: OK. I think I'm following so far. What's next?

WP: Our next measure of risk-adjusted returns, one of the most widely used, is the *Sharpe ratio (S$_i$)*, which is defined as

$$S_i = (R_i - R_f)/SD_i \,, \tag{3}$$

where SD_i is the standard deviation of asset i. As you can see, it's very similar to the Treynor ratio but uses the standard deviation as a measure of risk. The fourth column of Exhibit 7.2 shows the Sharpe ratios of the markets we're discussing, and at this point I shouldn't even ask whether you can reproduce how these numbers were calculated, right?

IS: Of course not! Staying with Chile, I have no trouble whatsoever in determining that its Sharpe ratio must have been calculated as $(0.161 - 0.04)/0.237 = 0.511$. That's easy. But why the standard deviation as a measure of risk instead of beta?

WP: Well, the Sharpe ratio aims to assess risk-adjusted returns by accounting for *total*, as opposed to just systematic risk. In a way, it's a more proper measure of risk-adjusted performance if you consider each asset in isolation.

IS: I see. And both ratios, Treynor and Sharpe, measure excess returns per unit of risk, so the only difference between them is how they define risk, right?

WP: Right. And because we're measuring excess returns per unit of risk, Sharpe ratios, just like Treynor ratios, lack intuition when calculated for an individual asset. Both are typically used to evaluate the *relative* performance of several assets and to rank them accordingly.

IS: Speaking of relative performance, Exhibit 7.2 shows that a ranking of the four emerging markets by the Sharpe ratio is different from the previous rankings by alpha and the Treynor ratio. In this case, Chile is the best performing market.

WP: Correct, and that shouldn't surprise you. As we said more than once before in this course, if you ask different questions you're likely to get different answers!

IS: Yes, I've learned that one for sure!

WP: Well, let's now move to our next measure of risk-adjusted returns. Interestingly, this next magnitude, called the **RAP**, an acronym for **risk-adjusted performance**, ranks assets in exactly the same way as does the Sharpe ratio.

IS: So why are we going to bother with it?

WP: Because, although a ranking of assets will always be the same with both measures, the RAP is expressed in percent and therefore is far more intuitive than the Sharpe ratio, even when calculated for an individual asset. But let's start with the definition; the RAP (RAP_i) is given by

$$RAP_i = R_f + (R_i - R_f)(SD_M/SD_i), \tag{4}$$

where SD_M is the standard deviation of the market, which in our example is the world market. The RAPs of the emerging markets we've been discussing are in the fifth column of Exhibit 7.2, and I barely dare ask you to reproduce those calculations by now!

IS: Not a problem. Going back to Chile, its RAP is $0.04 + (0.161 - 0.04)(0.143/0.237) = 11.3\%$. But how do we interpret this number? Expression (4) doesn't look straightforward to me.

WP: Well, at the very least, notice from expression (4) that the RAP of an asset increases with its return and decreases with its volatility. And even if the expression is not crystal clear, the intuition behind it is very neat. The RAP uses the volatility of the market as the reference point for risk. It then "punishes" assets riskier than the market by lowering their returns and "rewards" assets less risky than the market by increasing their returns.

IS: What's the point of "punishing" and "rewarding" assets?

WP: The point is to end up with figures in percent that are easy to interpret but that at the same time measure differences in risk-adjusted returns. Take Chile and Poland. Their mean returns were 16.1% and 18.4%, and their volatilities 23.7% and 34.4%. Since both markets were more volatile than the world market (14.3%), both will be "punished" with a decrease in their mean return; but because Poland is more volatile than Chile, it will be "punished" more severely.

IS: So the RAPs of both Chile and Poland should be lower than their mean returns.

WP: Exactly. And if you look at Exhibit 7.2, that's exactly what we find. Notice two things. First, the 16.1% return of Chile gets a 4.8% "punishment," leaving it with a RAP of 11.3%; but the 18.4% return of Poland gets a much higher 8.4% "punishment," leaving it with a RAP of just 10.0%. Second, although Poland outperforms Chile in terms of returns, once we factor in their differential risk, Chile outperforms Poland in terms of risk-adjusted returns.

IS: That's very interesting. But what exactly is the difference between the 11.3% and 10.0% RAPs of Chile and Poland?

WP: It's a difference in risk-adjusted returns, that is, a difference in returns but taking into account their differential volatility. Let me put it a different way. If investors cared only about returns, then, because Poland outperformed Chile by 2.3% a year, Poland would have been a better choice than Chile. But investors care about *both* returns and risk, and ultimately about risk-adjusted returns, and because Chile outperformed Poland by 1.3% a year, then Chile would have been a better choice than Poland. That, of course, is as long as you agree that the standard deviation is the proper way to assess risk.

IS: I think I understand. But looking at Exhibit 7.2 we see that all four countries are more volatile than the world market and therefore the RAP "punishes" them all. I assume it's also possible to "reward" assets, right?

WP: Right. Notice that in this example we're dealing with emerging markets, which are particularly volatile, so it shouldn't come as a surprise that they're riskier than the world market. But yes, it's perfectly possible to "reward" assets so that they end up with a RAP higher than their return.

IS: Gotcha. What's next?

WP: Our last measure of risk-adjusted returns, which most people call the **Sortino ratio (N_i)**, is given by

$$N_i = (R_i - B)/SSD_{Bi}, \tag{5}$$

where B is a benchmark chosen by the investor and SSD_{Bi} is the semideviation of asset i with respect to the benchmark B.

IS: That looks like the Treynor and Sharpe ratios, except for how excess returns are defined and how risk is measured.

WP: Exactly. We measure excess returns not necessarily with respect to the risk-free rate but with respect to any benchmark B chosen by the investor. And we assess risk with the semideviation with respect to the same benchmark B, therefore capturing volatility below this number. And if I may ask one last time, can you reproduce the calculations that lead to the numbers shown in the last column of Exhibit 7.2?

IS: The benchmark B used was a risk-free rate of 4%, right?

WP: Right, that makes it easier to compare with the other magnitudes we calculated.

IS: Then it's easy. Sticking with Chile, its Sortino ratio is $(0.161 - 0.04)/0.165 = 0.733$. And because this and the other Sortino ratios measure excess returns per unit of risk, I'm guessing that these ratios have little intuition and they're mostly used to rank relative performance, right?

WP: That's correct. And don't be fooled by Exhibit 7.2; although in this case Sharpe ratios and Sortino ratios would produce the same ranking of assets, it doesn't have to be the case. Exhibit 7.3 shows the Sharpe and Sortino ratios of Chile, plus those of Thailand and Malaysia, both also calculated over the 1998–2007 period, and, as you can see, the rankings get reversed once we change the measure of risk-adjusted returns.

IS: Well, I can only say that if you ask different questions you're likely to get different answers! Risk defined as volatility or as volatility below a chosen benchmark, as we discussed in a previous session, may lead to very different assessments.

WP: Exactly! So, any final questions before we wrap up for the day?

IS: Just one question. It seems to me that this whole idea of calculating risk-adjusted returns should have a critical impact on the widely used and abused expression "beating the market." Because beating the market in the short term or in the long term, on the basis of returns or risk-adjusted returns, are all very different things.

WP: Very insightful! You're absolutely right, so let me make a couple of quick points about that. First, beating

Exhibit 7.3

Market	Sharpe	Market	Sortino
Chile	0.511	Malaysia	0.832
Thailand	0.477	Thailand	0.792
Malaysia	0.476	Chile	0.733

or not beating the market in the short term may only reflect that we got lucky or unlucky. Second, beating the market in the long term should be possible simply by taking on more risk than the market. So, although we often hear that this or that fund manager beat the market last quarter or last year, that means very little. What really counts is whether we can beat the market, *on a risk-adjusted basis, consistently over the long term.* And, when it comes down to that, the evidence on our ability to pull it off is very damning.

IS: I'll never use the expression "beating the market" loosely again! Wrap-up time?

WP: You bet. A proper ranking of assets should pay little attention to the short term and not consider just returns; it should focus on the long term and on risk-adjusted returns. The focus on the long term is to avoid the impact of luck; the focus on risk-adjusted returns is to account for risk, which investors do care about. Because risk can be defined in more than one way, there are different measures of risk-adjusted returns; but we should avoid the temptation of highlighting one as better than the others. At the end of the day, because investors assess risk in different ways, they may end up ranking assets in different ways. And that is as far as we're going today!

Tool 8
NPV and IRR

This chapter discusses the two most widely used tools for project evaluation: NPV and IRR. Both tools require a critical input, the cost of capital, one of the most essential magnitudes for any company, which is also briefly discussed. Both NPV and IRR have applications that go way beyond project evaluation, and no toolbox would be complete without them.

Witty Professor (WP): Today we'll discuss a topic that we could have discussed at the very beginning, or we could have left for the very end, but the one thing we couldn't have done would be to skip it. I know some of you may be aware of these tools, but I want to make sure that we discuss here some important points about them.

Insightful Student (IS): Why are these tools so important?

WP: Well, to start with, companies create value only when they invest in "good" projects, which cannot be accurately done without the two tools we'll discuss today. But project evaluation is just one application of these tools; their scope really is much broader than that. Let me give you two quick examples. The discounted cash flow (DCF) model, which lies at the very heart of asset pricing, is just a variation of one of the two tools we'll discuss today. And the yield to maturity, the main magnitude used to assess the return of bonds, is simply the name given in bond pricing to the other tool we'll discuss today.

IS: Let's go for it then!

WP: All right, I'll start with an easy question: If I were to give you a million dollars, would you rather have it today or a year from today?

IS: What kind of question is that? Today, of course!

WP: Why?

IS: Well, simply because if you give me a million dollars today I'd deposit it safely in the bank, and a year from today I'd have more than a million dollars.

WP: Good. Second question: If I were to give you a million dollars, would you rather have it one year from today, two years from today, or three years from today?

IS: One year from today, of course, and for a similar reason. I could deposit in the bank the one million you give me one year from today and have more than one million two and three years from today. Just keep the easy questions coming!

WP: Well, you'll see in a minute the point of these simple questions, but for now just answer a third one: If I offered you either one million dollars for certain, or the flip of a coin such that heads I give you two million dollars and tails I give you nothing, what would you choose?

IS: One million dollars for certain. The prospect of getting two million dollars is great, but the possibility of getting nothing is too painful, so I'd take the certain one million.

WP: Just to make sure that you're thinking about this correctly, what are the probabilities of heads and tails, and therefore of getting two million or nothing?

IS: If the coin is fair, they're simply 50–50; I get two million with a probability of 50% and nothing with a probability of 50%.

WP: Exactly. Then, the so-called *expected value* of my offer is one million dollars, which we can calculate as (0.50)($2m) + (0.50)($0) = $1m. And between this expected value of one million dollars, and one million dollars for certain, you said you prefer the latter, right?

IS: Right.

WP: OK, now let's go back and state the three basic principles that follow from your answers. First, $1 today is worth more than $1 in the future. Second, $1 in the future is worth more than $1 in a more distant future. And third, a certain $1 is worth more than an uncertain or risky $1. Do you agree with these three principles?

IS: I do, they seem to be based on common sense.

WP: They are, and they are also embedded in the concept of *discounting*, which is at the heart of many financial calculations. If we *discount* a cash flow to be received in the future at an appropriate discount rate, we obtain its *present value*; that is, how much that future cash flow is worth to us today.

IS: And how do we get the appropriate discount rate?

WP: We'll talk about that in a few minutes, but before we get to that point let me introduce an essential financial concept. Given an investment or asset expected to deliver cash flows CF_1, CF_2, ..., CF_T in periods 1 through T, its **present value** (PV) is given by

$$PV = \frac{CF_1}{(1+DR)} + \frac{CF_2}{(1+DR)^2} + ... + \frac{CF_T}{(1+DR)^T}, \qquad (1)$$

where DR is the discount rate that captures the risk of those cash flows.

IS: Can you explain that expression a bit? It doesn't look very straightforward.

WP: Sure, though it is less difficult than it looks. On the numerators we simply have the cash flows we expect to receive over time; on the denominators we have the magnitude $(1 + DR)$ raised at the number of periods away from today those cash flows are. Notice that the farther away a cash flow is, the higher the power at which we raise $(1 + DR)$, and therefore the higher the discount factor we apply to it. That is consistent with the ideas that $1 today is worth more than $1 in the future, and that $1 in the future is worth more than $1 in a more distant future.

IS: Hold on a sec, explain that again please.

WP: Well, suppose that the discount rate is 12%. The discount factor for the first term is (1.12); for the second term it's $(1.12)^2 = 1.25$; for the third term it's $(1.12)^3 = 1.40$; and so forth. So, the farther away a cash flow is, the more we discount it, and the less it is worth to us today.

IS: Got it. Please continue.

WP: So far we established that the concept of present value reflects two of the basic principles we mentioned before: $1 today is worth more than $1 in the future, and $1 in the future is worth more than $1 in a more distant future.

IS: What about the third principle, that a certain $1 is worth more than a risky $1? Is it taken into account in this present value concept?

WP: It is, because the riskier an investment or asset is, the higher its discount rate will be. Which, by the way, is just another way to say, as we discussed in one of our previous sessions, that the riskier an investment or asset is, the higher is the return we require from it. In other words, higher risk implies a higher required return, a higher discount rate, and therefore a lower present value. Does it make sense?

IS: It does.

WP: Good, because then we're ready to define the first of the two tools we'll discuss today, which is just a tiny variation of the present value concept we just discussed. The *net present value* (NPV) of an investment is given by

$$\text{NPV} = -CF_0 + \frac{CF_1}{(1+DR)} + \frac{CF_2}{(1+DR)^2} + \dots + \frac{CF_T}{(1+DR)^T}, \quad (2)$$

which differs from the present value concept only in that here we have an initial cash flow that occurs at the present time, and for that reason it's not discounted.

IS: What is that initial cash flow?

WP: It's usually thought of as the initial investment required to start a project, and it's often written with a negative sign to highlight that it's usually a cost. But strictly speaking, neither the first cash flow has to be negative nor all the subsequent cash flows have to be positive.

IS: Why not?

WP: Well, think of an executive-education program like those run at most business schools. In most of those programs, the school first charges participants and then incurs the costs of delivering the program; therefore, the first cash flow is positive. On the other hand, think of a pharmaceutical company, which has to invest in R&D for many years before a drug gets to the market; in that case, not just the first but the first several cash flows will be negative.

IS: I see, but can you explain a bit the intuition behind the NPV concept?

WP: Sure, but the reason we spent a bit of time on those three basic principles is precisely because they are reflected on this NPV calculation. A project is expected to generate cash outflows and inflows over time, and we established that the farther away these cash flows are, the less they are worth to us today. We also established that the higher the risk of a project, the higher the discount rate should be, and therefore the less the cash flows are worth to us today. Put both ideas together and you have what a net present value calculation is all about: *Adjusting the expected cash flows of a project by their risk and timing to determine how much they are worth to us today.*

IS: So the resulting figure of this NPV calculation is expressed in current dollars, right?

WP: Exactly. Dollars received at different points in time are worth differently to us today, so we need to express all those cash flows in a common denominator, which is current dollars.

IS: OK, I think I understand, but an example certainly would help.

WP: And it's coming up. But for now let me ask you how you would use this NPV approach to evaluate whether or not to go ahead with an investment project.

IS: Well, given that we're adjusting expected cash flows by their risk and timing and expressing them all in current dollars, it seems to me that if the NPV of a project is positive then the project pays its way, so to speak, and therefore we should invest in it. Alternatively, if the NPV is negative, then for the opposite reasons we should not invest in it.

WP: That's exactly right, so let me formalize a bit that idea. The NPV approach simply says that given an investment project,

> *If NPV > 0 ⇒ Invest in the project*
> *If NPV < 0 ⇒ Do not invest in the project.*

IS: What if we're considering more than one project?

WP: As long as a project has a positive NPV, a company should invest in it. Having said that, if for some reason the company's capital is constrained and you have to choose among projects with positive NPVs, obviously you'd first choose the one with the highest NPV, then the one with the second-highest NPV, then the one with the third highest NPV, and so forth until the company runs out of the capital earmarked for investment projects.

IS: I'd still like to see an example, but it seems to me that this NPV approach is rather easy to implement.

WP: Well, as usual, the devil is in the details. Throwing a whole bunch of numbers into expression (2) and obtaining the resulting number is easy; but estimating correctly the cash flows of a project is, of course, extremely tricky and a bit of a mix of art and science.

IS: Yes, I can see that as being quite difficult. Is that any easier with the other tool? You said at the beginning of the session that we'd discuss two tools today.

WP: And we'll talk about the other one right now, but no, it doesn't solve the problem of having to estimate the expected cash flows of a project; you still need to do that. In any case, our second tool is the so-called *internal rate of return* (**IRR**), which is the discount rate that sets the NPV of a project equal to 0; that is,

$$\text{NPV} = -CF_0 + \frac{CF_1}{(1+\text{IRR})} + \frac{CF_2}{(1+\text{IRR})^2} + \dots + \frac{CF_T}{(1+\text{IRR})^T} = 0 \quad (3)$$

IS: So we start with the cash flows we expect from the project and solve for the discount rate that sets the NPV equal to 0. I understand that, but solving expression (3) is not easy at all! I could manage to find the IRR of a two-period project, maybe, but beyond that forget it!

WP: That's right, finding the IRR is not trivial from a mathematical point of view, but all financial calculators, and certainly Excel, can find it for you in the blink of an eye.

IS: How do we do that in Excel?

WP: We'll talk about that, but first, tell me, beyond its mathematical interpretation of being the discount rate that sets the NPV of a project equal to 0, can you see any other way to interpret the IRR?

IS: I'm not sure; it's not quite clear from expression (3).

WP: And that's precisely why I ask: to clarify the concept. *The IRR is the mean compound return expected from investing in a project*; that, of course, given the estimate of the project's expected cash flows.

IS: That's easy to understand; expression (3) suggested a more scary definition!

WP: I know, but that's both the correct and the most intuitive way to think of this magnitude. Now tell me, how would you use the IRR approach to decide whether or not to go ahead with an investment project?

IS: Well, it seems to me that I'd need to compare the IRR to something else, but I'm not sure to what.

WP: You're right, we need a benchmark rate to compare the IRR to, and the usual benchmark is a company's cost of capital, often referred to as the WACC, an acronym for the weighted-average cost of capital. Then, given an investment project,

> *If IRR > WACC ⇒ Invest in the project.*
> *If IRR < WACC ⇒ Do not invest in the project.*

IS: But why is the benchmark the cost of capital?

WP: The cost of capital is a company's hurdle rate; that is, the *minimum* return it should require from its projects. And this is the case because the cost of capital also is what it costs a company to raise capital. Therefore, if you're considering a project from which you expect a return higher than the cost of raising the funds to invest in it, you should obviously go for it. Wouldn't you be a happy shareholder if your company could raise money at 10% and invest it at 15%? On the contrary, if you expect from a project a lower return than the cost of raising the funds to invest in it, you obviously wouldn't want to go for it; raising money at 15% and investing it at 10% doesn't sound like good business, does it?

IS: I see. But I still have some questions, three in fact.

WP: Shoot!

IS: First, is the benchmark rate used to compare to the IRR always the company's cost of capital? What if, for example, two projects have very different levels of risk? Should we still use the same cost of capital as the discount rate for both?

WP: Good question, though I'm not sure I can give you a straightforward answer. This issue is actually somewhat controversial. Some would answer yes, arguing along the lines we did a minute ago. But others would argue that each project should have its own discount rate, related to each project's risk, which should be used to calculate each project's NPV or to compare to each project's IRR. The larger the difference in risk across projects, the more plausible this second point of view gets.

IS: But how different does the risk across projects have to be to make this second point of view plausible enough to get implemented?

WP: As you might guess, there is no precise answer to that. The devil, you probably realized by now, is usually in the details.

IS: Second question then: For any given project, do the NPV and IRR approaches always point in the same direction? In other words, do they always recommend the same decision about whether or not to invest in a project?

WP: Another good question! They often do, but it doesn't have to be the case. The IRR is a very intuitive magnitude but it also has some shortcomings. It's beyond the scope of our discussion to get into them but let me at least stress that whenever you have the NPV and the IRR approaches pointing in different directions, you should rely on the recommendation from the NPV approach.

IS: I'm curious about the shortcomings of the IRR but I understand we have time constraints and that we need to stick to the essentials. So, third question, how do we calculate a company's cost of capital?

WP: Let's briefly talk about that. And let's first assume that we're considering a company fully financed by equity, in which case it's all very simple: We calculate the company's cost of equity, or required return on equity, with the CAPM, and that will also be the company's cost of capital. In other words, if all the company's capital is equity, then the cost of capital is equal to the cost of equity, and we know how to calculate the latter with the CAPM.

IS: But many companies do use debt; what if that's the case?

WP: Unlike the cost of equity, which must be estimated with some model like the CAPM, the cost of debt is observable. If a company typically issues bonds, the market provides the yields to maturity at any point in time; and if a company typically borrows from a bank, the bank can provide the borrowing rate at any point in time.

IS: Hold on, what is a bond's yield to maturity?

WP: We'll talk about bonds in our last session, but for now it's enough to say that a bond's yield to maturity is the bond's internal rate of return, or mean compound return, that results from buying the bond at the market price and holding it until maturity. In other words, it's the return the market is requiring from the company's bonds at any given time.

IS: OK, so we can estimate the cost of equity with the CAPM, and we can observe the cost of debt from the market or a bank. That's easy. And then?

WP: Then you need to calculate how much the company is using of each source of capital, measured at *market* value and *relative* to the total capital used for investment purposes. In other words, you need to calculate the proportions in which the company is using debt and equity, both based on the market value of debt and equity.

IS: OK, that doesn't sound too difficult either. Anything else?

WP: Two things. First, you need to take into account that companies pay their corporate taxes after deducting interest payments on the debt. In other words, interest payments are tax deductible, which means that debt is somewhat cheaper than its actual cost indicates. If this is not very clear now it will hopefully be when we work out an example in just a minute.

IS: OK, and the second thing?

WP: Simply that you need to take into account that many companies use more than two sources of capital; they may also raise funds with instruments like preferred stock or convertible debt, among many others. You don't have to worry about these or other more complicated financial instruments. You only need to know that for each source of capital a company uses you still need the same two things, its cost or required return and its proportion of the total capital used for investment purposes.

IS: Got that. Then?

WP: Finally you simply calculate a weighted average of those costs, where the weights are the proportions we just mentioned. Just to formalize all this, let's consider a company that uses only debt and equity. Then, its weighted-average cost of capital (WACC) is given by

$$\text{WACC} = (1 - t_c) \cdot x_D \cdot R_D + x_E \cdot R_E, \qquad (4)$$

where R_D and R_E are the costs of debt and equity, the latter typically calculated with the CAPM; x_D and x_E are the proportions of debt and equity, measured at market value; and t_c is the corporate tax rate.

IS: And that $(1 - t_c)$ is the term that accounts for the tax advantage of debt, right?

WP: That's right. It simply says that although the cost of debt is R_D, what the company is effectively paying after taking the tax deduction into account is $(1 - t_c) \cdot R_D$, which is obviously lower than R_D.

IS: I think we're more than ready for an example!

WP: And here it comes! We're going to consider Boeing, the company that manufactures commercial aircraft, and we're going to put ourselves in their shoes when they were considering whether or not to start production of the 777 plane. And, I should add, we're going to simplify *very* substantially both their cost of capital and their calculation of the expected cash flows of the 777.

IS: Cool example! Let's go for it!

WP: Well, let's start by taking a look at Exhibit 8.1, which summarizes, in Panel A, some data necessary for the calculation of Boeing's cost of capital; and in Panel B, the cash flows expected from the 777 plane.

IS: How are those cash flows calculated?

WP: For our purposes let's just say that they are an educated best guess, taking into account all relevant costs and benefits for the company over the plane's expected lifetime. In other words, they are estimates of all the cash the company will invest in and receive from the 777 plane over its lifetime. And, importantly, let me

Exhibit 8.1

Panel A: Cost of capital		Panel B: Expected cash flows	
		Period	CF
Cost of debt (R_D):	10%		
Cost of equity (R_E):	13%	0	−$5,205m
Corporate tax rate (t_c):	34%	1	$1,749m
Debt (D):	$300m	2	$1,469m
Equity (E):	$15,000m	3	$2,327m
Long-term capital ($D + E$):	$15,300m	4	$2,724m

Source: All figures adapted from "The Boeing 777" case (UVA-F-1017); "m" indicates millions.

add that I've simplified those cash flows, which originally extended over a 35-year period, very substantially. Now, how about if we start by calculating Boeing's cost of capital? Could you do that?

IS: I think so, but one quick question first. Is that cost of equity estimated with the CAPM?

WP: Yes, it is.

IS: OK, so here we go then. Given that the total capital for investment purposes is $15,300 million, then the proportion of debt must be $300m/$15,300m = 2% and the proportion of equity must be $15,000m/$15,300m = 98%. Then, the cost of capital must be

$$WACC = (1 - 0.34)(0.02)(0.10) + (0.98)(0.13) = 12.9\%,$$

which is almost the same as the cost of equity.

WP: And that should come as no surprise from a company that finances its investments with 98% equity and 2% of debt, right?

IS: Right, no surprise there. But how should we interpret this 12.9%?

WP: The cost of capital can be interpreted in more than one way. The 12.9% figure can be thought of as a hurdle rate; that is, the minimum return required on Boeing's projects. Or it can be thought of as the company's average cost of raising funds for investments. So, given that Boeing's cost of raising funds in 1990 is 12.9%, they should obviously not accept any project that is expected to return less than that. Now, can you calculate the NPV of the 777 plane?

IS: I think so. Given a cost of capital of 12.9%, assuming that the full costs of the plane have to be paid up front, and that the following four cash flows are received at the end of each of the next four years, the NPV of the 777 plane should be

$$\text{NPV} = -\$5,205\text{m} + \frac{\$1,749\text{m}}{1.129} + \frac{\$1,469\text{m}}{1.129^2}$$

$$+ \frac{\$2,327\text{m}}{1.129^3} + \frac{\$2,724\text{m}}{1.129^4} = \$794\text{m},$$

which is almost $800 million.

WP: Exactly! And what do you make out of that number?

IS: Well, given that the 777 plane has a positive NPV, Boeing should go for it.

WP: Correct. And what about the project's IRR? Can you calculate it?

IS: I know how to set up the expression to calculate it, which should be

$$NPV = -\$5,205m + \frac{\$1,749m}{(1+IRR)} + \frac{\$1,469m}{(1+IRR)^2}$$

$$+ \frac{\$2,327m}{(1+IRR)^3} + \frac{\$2,724m}{(1+IRR)^4} = \$0 \quad ,$$

but I don't know how to solve for it.

WP: That's OK. The expression you set up is correct, and Excel could calculate the IRR for you in a split second, as we'll see in our additional optional session on some useful Excel commands. But for the time being let's just say that the IRR of this project is 19.4%.

IS: And because the IRR of 19.4% is higher than the cost of capital of 12.9%, the IRR approach agrees with the NPV approach in that Boeing should go ahead with this plane, right?

WP: Exactly. Just remember, though, that this doesn't have to be the case. The two approaches may occasionally point in different directions, and, like we said before, whenever that's the case you should rely on the recommendation of the NPV approach.

IS: Yes, I got that, and you did say that we're not going to discuss the problems the calculation of the IRR may have. But can you at least tell us what those problems may be?

WP: Sure. You may find cases in which it's simply not possible to find an IRR because there is no mathematical solution for expression (3). Or you may find cases in which you may have multiple IRRs, all of them being possible solutions to expression (3). Or you may find cases in which a lower IRR is better than a higher IRR, which could happen for more than one reason. Or you may find cases in which a project may have a higher IRR than another in some range but a lower IRR in some other range.

IS: Wow! And I thought the IRR would be easy to use!

WP: Don't get me wrong. I'm not suggesting that whenever you calculate the IRR of a project you're going to run into the problems I just mentioned. All I'm saying is that those problems are possible and that it's useful to be aware that they may occur. The IRR is a very useful and widely used magnitude, but, like any tool, it should be handled with care.

IS: With two minutes to go it looks like there's only time to wrap up!

WP: Here we go then. Companies create value when they invest in "good" projects and stay away from "bad" ones. NPV and IRR are the main two tools used for the formal evaluation of investment projects, although their usefulness actually extends way beyond this application. The cost of capital, a hurdle rate or minimum return required on the projects of a company, is a critical input in the implementation of both tools. The IRR is widely used, intuitive, and useful, but its calculation is subject to some potential problems; for that reason, whenever the NPV and IRR approaches point in different directions, NPV is the tool to rely on. And with my two minutes gone, I'd better let you go and take your well-deserved break!

Tool 9
Multiples

This chapter discusses stock valuation using relative valuation ratios, typically referred to as multiples. These multiples are widely used by equity analysts and widely discussed in the financial press. Their popularity is largely due to their simplicity, but, as discussed below, this simplicity may be deceiving and may lead to faulty analyses and, ultimately, to wrong investment decisions.

Witty Professor (WP): Although this is not a course on valuation, today we'll discuss a tool that is very widely used for the valuation of stocks. And the reason we will discuss it is twofold. First, because it is widely reported and discussed in the financial press, so it'll help you understand discussions you may often read or hear about. And second, because this tool is very often used in a simplistic way, which may lead you to make wrong investment decisions.

Insightful Student (IS): And what is the name of the tool we'll discuss?

WP: This tool goes by more than one name; some call it relative valuation ratios, though much more often you may see it simply referred to as multiples.

IS: Why relative valuation?

WP: The tools used in the valuation of stocks can be divided into two categories. The first, which we could call tools of absolute valuation, basically consist of different versions of the discounted cash flow (DCF) model. The second, which we could call tools of relative valuation, basically consist of ratios, more often than not between price and a fundamental variable expressed on a per-share basis.

IS: Hold on, what is a fundamental variable?

WP: Fundamental variables, sometimes simply referred to as fundamentals, are the value drivers of a company, those that determine how much a company is worth. Variables such as sales, earnings, cash flow, and dividends, among others, all qualify as fundamentals.

IS: Got it. So you were saying?

WP: I was about to say that absolute valuation models focus on the fundamentals of a company and value its stock on the basis of such fundamentals. Relative valuation ratios, on the other hand, value a company relative to something else, which in general we'll call a benchmark.

IS: So a company is cheap, expensive, or properly valued relative to that benchmark?

WP: Exactly, but let's not get ahead of our story. Let me first ask you whether you know any multiples.

IS: I know the price-to-earnings ratio, or P/E ratio, which I often see discussed in the financial press.

WP: Good. Other widely used multiples are the price-to-book ratio (P/B), the price-to-cash-flow ratio (P/CF), the price-to-dividend ratio (P/D), and the price-to-sales ratio (P/S), among others. And they usually have the current stock price in the numerator and a per-share fundamental variable, like earnings, book value, cash flow, dividends, or sales in the denominator.

IS: So how should we interpret these multiples?

WP: Just a second. Let me first propose that we focus the rest of the discussion on just one multiple, the P/E ratio, and this for three reasons. First, it is the most widely used. Second, it will make our lives easier not having to repeat each argument several times. And third, just about everything we'll say for the P/E, perhaps with a little tweaking here and there, is valid for the other multiples. Having said that, take a look at Exhibit 9.1, which shows some information on Abbott, Bristol-Myers Squibb (BMS), Johnson & Johnson (J&J), Merck, and Pfizer, all drug companies.

IS: Can you explain the exhibit a bit? At what point in time were those prices taken? What is a trailing EPS or a trailing P/E? What is the time period for those growth rates? What is a PEG?

Exhibit 9.1

	Abbott	BMS	J&J	Merck	Pfizer	Industry
Price	57.9	21.5	71.7	34.8	19.2	N/A
Trailing EPS	2.7	1.1	4.1	2.3	1.3	N/A
Trailing P/E	21.4	19.5	17.5	15.1	14.8	15.7
Growth (%)	11.4	10.6	8.0	6.2	5.0	7.9
PEG	1.9	1.8	2.2	2.4	3.0	2.0

WP: Sure, I was coming to that. All prices represent what you had to pay, in dollars, for a share of stock of each of these companies in early September 2008. "EPS" stands for earnings per share and "trailing" simply means that these are observed or past earnings; in this particular case, these are earnings per share over the preceding 12 months.

IS: Hold on a second. Why do we bother to add "trailing" to those EPS? Aren't the EPS always those the company already paid?

WP: Not necessarily. Analysts often forecast the EPS they expect companies to pay over the next quarter or next year, and even over longer periods. Those forecasted or expected EPS are usually referred to as "forward" EPS. Just to give you an example, J&J has trailing EPS of $4.1, shown in the exhibit, and forward EPS for the fiscal year 2009 of $4.7, not shown in the exhibit.

IS: So, whenever I see a P/E, how do I know whether it's based on trailing or forward EPS?

WP: Sometimes they are simply referred to as trailing or forward P/Es. But if that's not the case, you have to make sure you find out. It may be written in a foot-note, or at the bottom of a table, or if you're discussing P/Es with someone else and it's not clear to you, just ask. In fact, let me make a more general point: Because it can be so many different things, *always* make sure you know what the "E" part of the P/E is.

IS: What do you mean?

WP: I mean that the "P" part of the P/E is trivial; it's just the market price at a given point in time. But the "E" part is far trickier. It's not only that EPS can be trail-ing or forward, it goes way beyond that. Some analysts subtract one-time charges from the earnings and some others don't; some use as-reported earnings and others use operating earnings; and if you're making inter-national comparisons, different accounting standards define earnings in very different ways. The reasons why earnings are not a straightforward number are many and varied, and for our purposes you don't need to worry too much about that, but do keep in mind that you always need to know what the "E" of every P/E really is.

IS: Will do. So, going back to the exhibit now, we know what the "price" and "trailing EPS" rows show. What about the other rows?

WP: Well, the following row is simply the ratio between the previous two, and we call them "trailing" P/Es sim-ply because they're based on trailing EPS. And now let me ask you, how would you interpret those P/Es?

IS: I'd say they are the number of dollars we have to pay per dollar of EPS. In the case of BMS, for example, the

P/E of 19.5 indicates that we have to pay $19.5 per each $1 of this company's EPS.

WP: Exactly! That's the correct way to think about P/Es. Now, second question, going back to BMS, what does this P/E of 19.5 mean in terms of valuation? Is BMS cheap? Expensive? Properly valued?

IS: No idea. I don't know whether 19.5 is high, or low, or right on the mark.

WP: And the point of my question is, precisely, that you realize that this 19.5 by itself is pretty useless. That's why P/Es are a tool of *relative* valuation; we need to put this number into perspective, relative to something else. Now, what would you compare that P/E to?

IS: The P/E of a competitor?

WP: It's a possibility. So what would you do?

IS: Well, I'd say that BMS (P/E = 19.5) is more expensive than Pfizer (P/E = 14.8) and cheaper than Abbott (P/E = 21.4).

WP: So?

IS: I'm not quite sure. I guess that given those P/Es, if I had to choose between BMS and Pfizer, I'd buy Pfizer; and if I had to choose between BMS and Abbott, I'd buy BMS.

WP: Careful! This is precisely why I ask the question! Do you think that valuing stocks could be as easy as saying that 19.5 is higher than 14.8 and lower than 21.4! If that were the case, then we'd all be analysts. Even better, we'd all be rich!

IS: I'm not sure I follow you.

WP: What I'm saying is that the analysis you just made, which to be fair is similar to that often found in many financial newspapers and heard from some financial pundits on TV, is not simple; it's *simplistic*. Again, valuing stocks cannot be, and is not, as simple as saying that 19.5 is higher than 14.8 and lower than 21.4. You don't need any financial expertise to make that comparison.

IS: So what should we do instead?

WP: To start with, don't you think that comparing a company in which you may be interested, say BMS, to just one or two other companies is a little limited?

IS: Maybe. Are you suggesting that we should use more companies in the comparison?

WP: In part, yes. But let me make a more general argument. Whenever analysts are using multiples, they have two critical issues to deal with: First, they must determine the proper benchmarks for the comparison; and, second, they must determine why the multiple for the company they are analyzing and the chosen benchmarks may differ.

IS: And what is a proper benchmark?

WP: Let's talk about that first issue. There are three standard benchmarks that analysts tend to use, of which we'll focus on two. The two more widely used are often referred to as a *temporal* benchmark and a *cross-sectional* benchmark; the one we will not discuss is often referred to as a *theoretical* benchmark.

IS: Can you at least tell us what this last one is about?

WP: Sure. It basically consists of a model that tells you what the P/E of a company *should* be; you input the values of some variables on one end and you get the "appropriate" P/E on the other end. Needless to say, there is not just one but several models for this purpose.

IS: Got it. What about the temporal and the cross-sectional benchmarks?

WP: The *temporal benchmark* is used to assess the current valuation of a company relative to its historical valuation, and you calculate it simply by taking the company's average P/E over the past several years.

IS: What's the point of the comparison?

WP: The point is that if a company and the environment surrounding it have not changed substantially over time, its valuation shouldn't have changed too much either. In other words, similar conditions call for similar valuations.

IS: But as you told us more than once before, the devil is in the details, right?! It's probably not trivial to assess whether we're comparing apples to apples or apples to oranges.

WP: Excellent point! You're absolutely right about that. And this is one of the many reasons why relative valuation is much more than a trivial comparison between two numbers and why analysts have a substantial contribution to make.

IS: I see. Can you give us an example of a temporal benchmark?

WP: Sure. Although it's not shown in Exhibit 9.1, I could tell you that between 1990 and 2007, the average P/E of BMS was 24.8, which is quite a bit higher than its current P/E of 19.5.

IS: And what do you make out of that?

WP: Not much. And it's important that you don't make too much out of that. As we said before, anybody can see that 19.5 is lower than 24.8, but you should not rush to conclude that BMS is undervalued. Obviously, some further analysis is necessary.

IS: And how many months or years should we use to calculate the average P/E?

WP: As you said a minute ago, the devil is in the details, right?! There is no way to say whether you should calculate the average over 10, 20, or more years. Ideally, you should go back enough years so that the average is not heavily influenced by one or two very good or very bad years. But you don't want to go so far back that the average is largely made up of P/Es from years in which the company was very different from what it is now. Here again an experienced analyst can make a substantial contribution.

IS: OK, what about the cross-sectional benchmark?

WP: The *cross-sectional benchmark* is used to assess the current valuation of a company relative to the current valuation of other comparable companies, and you calculate it simply by taking the average P/E of several of these comparable companies. The point of the comparison is, of course, that similar companies should have similar valuations.

IS: What is a comparable company?

WP: A company as similar as possible to the one you're analyzing. But, of course, this is just an ideal. In practice, as you might guess, comparable companies are hardly ever really comparable.

IS: Which means, again, that it's not trivial to tell whether we're comparing apples to apples or apples to oranges, right?

WP: Exactly. Going back to your previous comparison of the P/Es of BMS, Pfizer, and Abbott, I'm sure you would have a hard time arguing whether these three companies are really comparable to each other, although all three are drug companies.

IS: Yes, I think I would.

WP: Of course you would. Which explains why, very often, analysts tend to use broad cross-sectional benchmarks, such as the P/E of the industry of the company they're analyzing.

IS: And that would be the 15.7 shown in the last column of Exhibit 9.1, which is calculated on the basis of many more companies than those in the exhibit, right?

WP: That's right. And, as I hope it's clear by now, you should not rush to conclude that because the 19.5 P/E of BMS is higher than the 15.7 P/E of the industry, then BMS is overvalued.

IS: Yes, I understand that now. But I have two questions. First, which benchmark should we use, temporal or cross-sectional?

WP: That is not an either-or choice. In fact, the more benchmarks you use in your analysis the more robust it's going to be. Each would provide you with some perspective and give you some insight into the valuation of the company you're analyzing. Second question?

IS: I'm a bit puzzled by the fact that if we use a temporal benchmark, BMS is cheap relative to its historical valuation. However, if we use a cross-sectional benchmark, BMS is expensive relative to its peers. Is that possible?

WP: First, let me stress once again that those two comparisons are far from enough to conclude that BMS is overvalued or undervalued. Second, notice that when you use those two benchmarks you're asking two very different questions, so you should not necessarily expect the same answers. And third, if it happens to be the case that all your comparisons point in the same direction, then your conclusion will be stronger and more reliable; but if that doesn't happen, it at least invites the interesting question of why not, which again will strengthen your analysis.

IS: Gotcha.

WP: Good. Now, remember that we mentioned before that an analyst using multiples has two critical issues to deal with: Determining the proper benchmarks for the comparison, and determining why the multiple for the company he's analyzing and the chosen benchmarks may differ. Most of what we've been discussing so far is related to the first issue, so let's move on to the second issue now.

IS: If we're going to talk about why a given multiple and the chosen benchmarks may differ, can we go back to where we left the comparison between BMS (P/E = 19.5) and Abbott (P/E = 21.4)?

WP: Sure. And we'll also discuss, more generally, the comparison between a given multiple for a company and both a temporal and a cross-sectional benchmark. But let's start from where you propose. Earlier, when comparing BMS and Abbott, you had tentatively suggested that you'd be inclined to buy the former because it was cheaper, at least in terms of the price you had to pay relative to the EPS of the company, right?

IS: Right.

WP: And I had suggested in turn that your analysis was not simple but simplistic; that it requires no expertise whatsoever to say that 19.5 is lower than 21.4; and that valuing stocks must obviously be harder than that. Now think about where your argument comes from and to where it leads. First, it comes from assuming that these two companies must be worth the same; or, put differently, that they must have the same P/E. Second, if that were true, it leads to the perplexing conclusion that market participants are doing nothing about the discrepancy in P/Es; and that includes the thousands of very well-paid analysts whose main job is to find mispriced stocks and to let their clients know about them. How plausible is that?

IS: Now that you put it that way, not very plausible.

WP: OK, let's take my two points one at a time, the first one now and the second we'll leave for later. First, is it plausible to assume that these two companies must have the same P/E?

IS: Well, not really. Although they both belong to the same industry, they may have different growth expectations, different risk, and so forth. Actually, come to think of it, they may differ in a thousand ways so there's really no reason why they should have the same P/E.

WP: OK, but let's try to narrow down those "thousand ways" in which two companies may differ. As a matter of fact, you just suggested two of the main reasons why two companies may have a different valuation even if they belong to the same industry: growth expectations and risk. Therefore, when the P/E of the company you're analyzing and a given benchmark differ, the first thing you need to ask is whether the company and the benchmark have the same growth expectations and risk. And you should do that regardless of the type of benchmark you're using.

IS: I think I understand the general argument but can you give us an example?

WP: Sure. Let's go back to your comparison between BMS and Abbott and to your conclusion that BMS is a better buy. That's a conclusion you can't draw simply by comparing the P/Es of these two companies. Yes, BMS with a P/E of 19.5 is cheaper than Abbott with a P/E of 21.4. But isn't it possible that BMS is riskier than Abbott? Isn't it possible that Abbott is expected to grow faster than BMS? And if either of these two things or both were true, wouldn't it make sense to pay more for a company that is less risky or expected to grow faster than the other?

IS: I guess it would.

WP: It sure would. And that's why, when you get right down to it, a proper analysis with multiples always involves some fundamental analysis. You must analyze fundamentals to understand whether the differences in valuation you're observing in the market are justified or not.

IS: OK, let me see if I understand. You're saying, first, that we should stay away from simply comparing a P/E and a benchmark and draw from that comparison a conclusion about whether a company is mispriced or properly priced. You're also saying that we shouldn't do that because there may be good reasons why the P/E and the benchmark may differ, two of the main reasons being differences in expected growth and risk. And you're finally saying that when we start looking into those two and perhaps other fundamentals, at the end of the day we end up engaging in fundamental analysis. Bottom line, valuation with multiples may seem simple but at the end of the day, when done properly, it involves the analysis of fundamentals, which is very far from just comparing two numbers. Is that a fair summary of your points?

WP: It's a *fantastic* summary of my points! I would only add that you should always look at the comparison between a P/E and a benchmark as the *beginning*, not the end, of your analysis.

IS: Roger that, but I have a question. Suppose I'm considering a company, say BMS with its 19.5 P/E, and I'm using a temporal benchmark, like the 24.8 over the 1990–2007 period you mentioned before. So in order to try to explain the difference between these two P/Es I look into whether the growth expectations of BMS are better or worse than its past growth, or whether it's more or less risky than it's been in the past. And suppose that, to strengthen my analysis, I do something similar for a cross-sectional benchmark like the 15.7 on Exhibit 9.1, and I consider differences in growth expectations and risk between BMS and the other drug companies in the industry. What if I look into those and perhaps other fundamental variables and still can't explain the difference between the P/E of BMS and these benchmarks?

WP: Good question. When you do that comparison, you have two possible outcomes. One is that you do find the variable or variables that explain the difference in P/Es; you may find, for example, that BMS is now cheaper than it's been historically because the company is expected to grow in the future at a lower rate than it did in the past or is expected to be riskier than it's been in the past. In that case, then, there is no trading opportunity; that is, you did find out why the multiple and the benchmark differ and why the company is properly priced despite this difference.

IS: And if I can't find anything that explains the difference in P/Es?

WP: Well, in that case, you may have found a trading opportunity. If, after a thorough analysis, you were not able to explain the difference between a P/E and a benchmark, it is possible that the market is not valuing the company you're analyzing properly, in which case it's a good opportunity for you to trade and to take advantage of the mispricing. But you should always be careful, and even a bit skeptical, when you find yourself in this second case.

IS: Why?

WP: Well, whenever you conclude that a stock is cheap or expensive, and therefore a good stock to buy or sell, you have to ask why most investors in the market do not agree with you. And I say that they must not agree with you because if they did, they'd be doing the same trades that you have in mind, pushing prices in such a way as to eliminate the trading opportunity.

IS: Wait, wait, wait, I didn't get that last part. Can you explain that again?

WP: Sure. Suppose you think that a stock is cheap and therefore a good buy. And suppose that many investors share your view. Well, what they'd do is to buy shares in the company, pushing up its price, and giving you less reason to think that the stock is cheap. And, of course, as long as your assessment is the same as theirs, they'll keep buying until the market price reflects the price that both you and they think is the right one, at which point the stock will no longer be cheap but properly priced.

IS: And what if my assessment and their assessment of the "right" price is different?

WP: Well, then, we're sort of back to square one, and you have to wonder how it's possible that you have a better insight than that of many well-informed, well-connected, and very knowledgeable investors in the market.

IS: I see. So you're suggesting that we should not try to find mispriced stocks, right?

WP: Well, I wouldn't go that far. I guess what I'm suggesting is that you keep in mind what Peter Lynch, the venerable former manager of the Fidelity Magellan fund used to say: "What makes stock picking difficult…is that 1,000 people smarter than you are studying the same stocks you are." Sounds plausible?

IS: It sure does, particularly coming from one of the best stock pickers in history!

WP: Well, we seem to be running out of time. Any final questions?

IS: Two quick ones. First, more than once I've seen in the press a reference to something called the PEG ratio, which I also see in Exhibit 9.1. Can you at least very briefly explain that magnitude?

WP: Sure. The PEG is a multiple devised to account for the differences in expected growth between a company and a benchmark. It is simply the P/E ratio of a company divided by its expected growth; that is, PEG $=$ (P/E)/g, where g denotes the expected annual growth in EPS. Because, as we suggested earlier, a company may be more or less expensive than a benchmark simply because it is expected to grow faster or more slowly, the PEG incorporates this differential growth. And, of course, the lower the PEG, the more attractive the company, simply because a lower PEG indicates a cheaper company or one that is expected to grow more quickly.

IS: Can you give us a quick example?

WP: Sure. The last two rows of Exhibit 9.1 show the expected annual growth in EPS five years ahead and the PEG based on that expected growth. The PEG of BMS, for example, is simply calculated as 19.5/10.6 = 1.8. And notice something interesting: The naive comparison between the 19.5 P/E of BMS and the 15.7 P/E of the industry suggests that BMS is expensive relative to the industry. But note that BMS is expected to grow its EPS at 10.6% a year, much faster than the industry's 7.9%. Therefore, once you factor in this differential growth, the 1.8 PEG of BMS is lower than the 2.0

PEG of the industry, thus making BMS relatively more attractive than the industry. Do you see now how a simplistic comparison may be misleading?

IS: I do! But that's not the end of the analysis, is it? Because then we would have to inquire into differences in risk and other variables that may strengthen or weaken the conclusion that BMS is attractively priced relative to the industry.

WP: Exactly! I'm glad to see that you're beginning to grasp how to properly implement a valuation by multiples! Your second and final question?

IS: Simply that our whole discussion was from the perspective of valuing a company, but I assume that P/Es can be used in similar ways to value markets, right?

WP: Yes, good point. Just about everything we said about P/Es and the valuation of companies is also valid for the valuation of groups of companies, such as industries, sectors, regions, or markets, as long as you have an aggregate multiple for each of them.

IS: Ready for the wrap-up then!

WP: Good. Multiples, which are widely used by analysts and widely reported in the financial press, are used to value stocks or groups of stocks relative to one or more benchmarks. These multiples are often used in a simplistic way by naively comparing two numbers and drawing premature conclusions that may lead to wrong investment decisions. There may be good reasons why a multiple and a benchmark may differ, and differences in expected growth and risk are the main suspects. Once you start considering these and other variables, you end up engaging in fundamental analysis, at which point valuation by multiples ceases to be the simplistic comparison many seem to think it is. And, if I heard correctly, the bell that just rang suggests that our time is up for today!

Tool 10
Bonds

This final chapter discusses a financial instrument that governments, companies, and investors could hardly live without. Bonds are an essential asset class, widely used by governments and companies to finance their investments and by investors to protect their portfolios. They come in many types and degrees of complexity, but the simple bonds discussed here, whose characteristics of risk and return are not difficult to understand, are the most widely used.

Witty Professor (WP): We have finally come to the end of our course, and last, but certainly not least, we're going to discuss bonds, one of the most widely used financial instruments.

Insightful Student (IS): I guess we all read about them in the papers, but some of the terminology related to them is not very clear, at least to me. Can you start by briefly defining some of the basic terms?

WP: Sure, I was going to start with that. Think of a bond simply as a loan in which the issuer or seller is the borrower and the buyer is the lender. The issuer receives a lump sum when the bond is issued and promises to pay back the amount borrowed, called the *principal* or *face value*, at a specified point in time called the *maturity date*.

IS: But lending you $100 and getting back $100 at some point in the future doesn't sound like a great deal to me!

WP: And it's not. That's why between the time the bond is issued and the maturity date most bonds pay interest, typically twice a year. The interest is determined by the *interest rate*, also called the *coupon*, and is calculated with respect to the face value. All the relevant terms of the contract between the buyer and the seller are contained in a document called the bond's *indenture*.

IS: Can you please put a few numbers behind the concepts you just described?

WP: You bet. Suppose a company issues a 5-year bond today with a face value of $1,000 and an interest rate or coupon of 8%. That means the company receives $1,000 today, will pay back $1,000 five years from today, and will make five $80 payments in annual interest, typically split into two semiannual payments of $40 each. Is that clear?

IS: It is. But is the interest rate always fixed throughout the life of a bond?

WP: In the most common type of bonds, which are usually called *coupon bonds*, yes. But there are in fact bonds, which we'll leave out of our discussion, whose interest rate changes over time; they are called *floating-rate bonds*.

IS: And who can issue bonds?

WP: Governments and companies certainly can and do. But in fact just about anybody can issue a bond, as long as the promise to return the principal and make the interest payments is believable and the terms offered are attractive enough. As a matter of fact, even rock stars can issue bonds! Both David Bowie and Michael Jackson have done it in the past.

IS: Interesting!

WP: Now, you said before that you often read about bonds in the papers, and that is because once a bond is issued and bought by someone, that someone can sell it in the market later on, and anybody who buys it can in turn sell it too, and so forth. In other words, bonds trade in markets pretty much like stocks do.

IS: I've often seen the expression "trading at a premium" or "trading at a discount" but I don't quite understand what that means. At a premium or at a discount with respect to what?

WP: With respect to the face value of the bond. So if a company issued a bond with a face value of $1,000, when the bond trades at a price higher than $1,000, it is said to trade at a premium; and when it trades at a price lower than $1,000, it is said to trade at a discount. And just in case you ever see or hear the expression, when the bond trades at $1,000, it is said to trade "at par."

IS: Now, given that we know in advance all the cash flows we're going to receive, then pricing a bond should be relatively easy, right? It should just be a straightforward present value calculation, with the coupons and principal being the cash flows to be discounted.

WP: Well, it's true that all the cash flows are known in advance, but the risk of those cash flows is not trivial to assess. As we'll discuss in a few minutes, the probability of receiving those cash flows may vary substantially across issuers. Some issuers are more likely to default than others, and, of course, that differential risk should be reflected in the discount rate.

IS: So are we going to discuss how to calculate those discount rates?

WP: No, and for two reasons. First, that goes quite a bit beyond the basic issues we discuss in this course. And second, as an individual investor, when considering bonds you should focus less on their price and more on their return.

IS: But if we know the cash flows and the price we have to pay for them, then it seems to me that the return we get is just a straightforward IRR calculation, isn't it? It's pretty much like an investment project in which we have forecasts of the cash flows and we know the initial investment we have to make, with the obvious difference that the project's cash flows are expected and the bond's cash flows, default notwithstanding, are certain.

WP: Exactly! Very insightful! Precisely, the most widely used magnitude to describe the return of a bond is the *yield to maturity*, which is nothing but the IRR that you get by buying the bond at the market price and holding it until maturity.

IS: As usual, an example would help!

WP: And it's coming right up! By mid-September 2008, a 10-year note issued by the US government, with a face value of $100 and an interest rate of 4%, was trading at $104.9 and had a yield to maturity of 3.41%. And, as we mentioned before, although neither the face value nor the interest rate will change throughout the life of this bond, the market price and therefore the yield will change almost constantly.

IS: So, if we buy this 10-year bond at $104.9 and keep it until maturity, the 3.41% yield to maturity indicates our mean annual compound return if we hold the bond until it matures, right?

WP: Exactly. As we discussed earlier in this course, an internal rate of return is simply a mean annual compound return. And it's important that you keep in mind that that is the return we will receive if, and only if, we keep the bond until maturity.

IS: What if we sell the bond before maturity?

WP: Well, in that case, given that bond prices fluctuate over time, the price at which we sell the bond can be higher or lower than the price we paid for it, which means that, just like when we buy stocks, we can have a capital gain or a capital loss. Put differently, the return we get by selling the bond before maturity can be anything, including a negative return.

IS: A negative return?!

WP: Sure. The appropriate discount rate for the cash flows of a bond has the same two components we discussed earlier in the course, a risk-free rate and a risk premium, the former related to inflationary expectations and the latter related to risk. So, suppose inflationary expectations go up. Then discount rates will go up, and, given that a bond's cash flows are fixed, its price will necessarily go down.

IS: And I assume the same can happen if the risk premium goes up, right? For example, if a company becomes riskier, investors will increase the return required on its bonds, pushing discount rates up and bond prices down.

WP: Exactly. Whatever pushes discount rates up necessarily pushes bond prices down, and the other way around. So, although bonds are usually thought of as a safe investment, it *is* possible to lose money by investing in them. In fact, US bonds, the safest in the world, delivered negative returns both in 1999 and in 1994.

IS: I see. So the bottom line is that although it may be less likely than when investing in stocks, if we sell before maturity it is still possible to lose money when investing in bonds, right?

WP: That's correct. When you buy a bond at a given price and hold it until maturity, you lock a mean annual compound return indicated by the bond's yield to maturity. But if you sell anytime before maturity, then your return can be higher, lower, positive, or negative.

IS: Now, correct me if I'm wrong, but by holding a bond until maturity we can only lock a *nominal* return, right? Because not knowing what the inflation rate is going to be in the future, we still have uncertainty about the *real* return we're going to perceive. And if that's the case, then we still face uncertainty about our future purchasing power.

WP: That's right. Your nominal return is guaranteed, but your real return is not. Good point. In fact, although we will leave them out of our discussion, the US government issues some bonds called TIPS which do guarantee a real return.

IS: Interesting. Now, the nominal return of a bond is easy to assess with its yield to maturity, but what about its risk? Is it also easy to assess?

WP: Well, as usual, risk is more difficult to assess than return. And, as usual, risk comes from multiple sources. As far as bonds are concerned, though, the most important source is the so-called *default risk*, which is related to the probability that the issuer pays the coupons and principal it agreed to pay.

IS: But except in a few obvious cases, such as the US government, that probability must be very difficult to assess.

WP: It's not easy, particularly if you try to assess how much higher the probability of default of one issuer is compared to that of another issuer. But investors get help from rating agencies like Standard and Poor's or Moody's, whose main business is, precisely, to assess the probability of default of bonds and to communicate it to the market in a simple way that investors can easily understand.

IS: And that simple way consists of the famous credit ratings, right?

WP: Exactly. So what rating agencies essentially do is to assess default risk and to summarize their assessment in credit ratings.

IS: And what is a good credit rating or a bad credit rating?

WP: Each rating agency has its own way of rating bonds. The easiest to remember is the one used by Standard and Poor's which, from best to worst, is summarized by the letters AAA, AA, A, BBB, BB, B, CCC, CC, C, and D. The first four rating categories, from AAA to BBB, are called "investment grade bonds" and they are very unlikely to default. The rest of the categories, from BB to C, are called "high-yield (or 'junk') bonds," and have a much higher probability of default. The final category, D, simply indicates that the issuer has defaulted.

IS: So, as we move from AAA to C the probability of default increases, right?

WP: Right.

IS: And how reliable are these ratings? I ask because I've read more than one article in the press that suggest that rating agencies don't do such a great job.

WP: I'm glad you brought that up. In fact, many times in the past the reliability of credit ratings has been questioned. This is a very controversial issue, and we're obviously not going to resolve it here, but the consensus seems to be that rating agencies are pretty good at assessing the probability of default in the long term and, at the same time, are somewhat slow to react in the short term.

IS: What do you mean by "slow to react in the short term?"

WP: Think of Enron, for example, which was rated investment grade by the rating agencies until just four days before filing for bankruptcy! Or the bonds of some Asian countries during the 1997 crisis, which were downgraded to junk status after the really bad news hit the newspapers. Obviously, rating agencies are supposed to give *advance* warning of trouble not react *after* trouble becomes public.

IS: And what about in the long term?

WP: In the long term, and when assessing "plain-vanilla" bonds, rating agencies do a pretty good job. Take a look at Exhibit 10.1, which shows so-called mortality rates between 1971 and 2003 for corporate bonds. The second column shows, for each rating category, the proportion of principal that defaulted five years after the bonds were issued; the third column shows the

Exhibit 10.1

S&P Rating	5 Years (%)	10 Years (%)
AAA	0.03	0.03
AA	0.50	0.55
A	0.28	0.82
BBB	7.64	9.63
BB	12.17	19.69
B	28.32	37.26
CCC	47.30	58.63

Source: Adapted from Edward Altman and Gonzalo Fanjul, "Defaults and Returns in the High Yield Bond Market: The Year 2003 in Review and Market Outlook," Working Paper, 2004.

same proportions but ten years after issuance. What do you think?

IS: There does seem to be a very close relationship between ratings and mortality. Clearly, the worse the rating, the higher the default rate both five and ten years after issuance. Given that information, credit ratings look quite reliable to me.

WP: And they are, but just remember that this is a long term perspective and confined to "plain-vanilla" corporate bonds. Rating agencies have usually had more trouble defending their record in the short term and when rating more complicated types of debt, such as asset-backed securities or structured products more generally.

IS: What are asset-backed securities?

WP: Never mind – like I said, a more complicated type of debt. I'll go as far as to say that they basically consist of a group of many loans lumped together into a bond-like asset.

IS: Roger that. But it seems to me that one way to see whether market participants tend to rely on credit ratings when they assess the risk of bonds is to see whether, as credit ratings worsen, the yield that issuers have to pay increases.

WP: Good point. And it is indeed the case that there is a clear relationship between credit ratings and bond yields. In general, as the credit rating worsens, default risk increases, and so do the yields required by investors. You can check out the newspaper yourself and you'll see that as you move from AAA ratings down to C ratings issuers have to pay higher yields.

IS: Can you at least give us a quick example?

WP: Sure. Let's consider 5-year bonds in mid-September 2008. The AAA-rated bond of Pfizer had a yield of 4.62%; the BBB-rated bond of Home Depot had a yield of 5.32%; and the CCC-rated bond of Toys "R" Us had a yield of 12.75%. So, as you see, the lower the rating, the higher the yield.

IS: I see. But is there any difference between a yield and a spread? I seem to remember reading in the newspaper that as credit ratings worsen, spreads increase, which is similar to the relationship you're telling us between credit ratings and yields.

WP: A spread is simply the difference between the yield paid by any given issuer and the yield paid by the US government at the same maturity. If we go back to our previous example, and considering that the yield on

5-year US bonds in mid-September 2008, was 2.51%, then the spread on the Pfizer bond is 2.11% (= 4.62% – 2.51%); the spread on the Home Depot bond is 2.81% (= 5.32% – 2.51%); and the spread on the Toys "R" Us bond is 10.24% (= 12.75% – 2.51%). So, as you see, it is true that the lower the rating the higher the spread.

IS: Well, if the spread measures how much more an issuer has to pay relative to what the US government has to pay at the same maturity, then it does make sense that as we move from AAA-rated issuers to C-rated issuers spreads widen.

WP: It sure does.

IS: Now, it seems clear from our discussion that there is a very close relationship between credit ratings and yields; the worse the credit rating, the higher the yield an issuer has to pay, and the higher the return received by the buyer. Does that mean that default is the only relevant source of risk when evaluating a bond?

WP: Good question, and the answer is no. Yields and therefore returns are primarily driven by default risk, but there certainly are other relevant sources of risk. An important one is the so-called *market risk*, or *interest-rate risk*, and it basically measures the volatility of bond returns.

IS: So the higher the market risk, the higher the volatility, and the higher the bond yield?

WP: Yes, and a rough way to think about this market risk is that it increases as the maturity of the bond

increases. In general, given bonds of similar characteristics, the longer a bond's maturity, the higher the
market risk, and therefore the higher the yield it pays.
Have you ever heard about the yield curve?

IS: No, what is it?

WP: It's simply a relationship that shows the yield the US
government pays at each maturity. In general, but not
necessarily always, the yield curve is upward sloping,
which simply means that the longer the maturity, the
higher the yield. Exhibit 10.2 shows the yield curve for
US government bonds in mid-September 2008, and as
you can see it is indeed upward sloping.

IS: And you're saying that, in general, a longer maturity implies a higher volatility and, as a result, a higher
yield to compensate for the extra risk, right?

WP: Exactly.

IS: Are there any other important sources of risk that
should be considered when evaluating bonds?

WP: Default risk is by far the most important; keep that
in mind. And market risk does play a role in the deter-
mination of yields. Beyond that, there are many other

Exhibit 10.2

Maturity	Yield (%)
6 months	0.69
3 years	1.41
5 years	2.51
10 years	3.41
30 years	4.08

sources of risk that play less significant roles, and I'm going to mention only one: liquidity risk.

IS: What is that?

WP: Liquidity is not very easy to define but it is related to both the speed with which you can buy or sell an asset, as well as to the impact on prices when you buy or sell. The faster you can make a transaction, and the less you affect prices, then the more liquid is the asset.

IS: I can see that the more difficult it is for us to trade, the more risk we're going to perceive, and the higher the yield we're going to require. But I can't see why the impact on prices matters.

WP: Because when you want to execute a transaction in an illiquid market, prices always move in a direction that hurts you. If you want to buy an illiquid asset, its price will increase, perhaps substantially, which is, of course, not what you want. And if you want to sell an illiquid asset, its price will decline, perhaps substantially, which again is not what you want.

IS: And you're saying that the more illiquid the asset the more that that will happen, right?

WP: Right. That is why the more illiquid you perceive a bond to be, the higher the yield you will require to buy it.

IS: I think I'm beginning to understand what bonds are all about.

WP: That's good because this course is about to finish!

IS: But not before a wrap-up on bonds!

WP: Of course not, so here we go. Bonds are an essential asset class that governments and companies use to finance their investments and investors use to protect their portfolios. The most common bonds offer fixed interest payments and return the principal at maturity. The return obtained by buying a bond at the market price and holding it until maturity is given by its yield to maturity, which is simply the bond's internal rate of return. Risk, in turn, is primarily driven by default risk, which is related to the probability that the issuer makes the promised payments. Credit ratings play a crucial role in the assessment of credit risk and are widely used by investors. Finally, volatility and liquidity also contribute to the risk of bonds, and the higher they are, the higher the yield a bond has to offer.

IS: So, we've come to the end of the road!

WP: We have, and I hope that by now you have a better grasp of some essential financial tools that will help you understand better what you read or hear in the financial press and hopefully to participate more intelligently in financial discussions. If you achieved that, then this course was worth both your time and mine. And this, my dear insightful students, is as far as this course goes. Thanks and goodbye!

Appendix: Some Useful Excel Commands

This appendix discusses some useful Excel commands, restricting the scope to those related to the financial tools and concepts covered in this book. The commands are discussed in pretty much the same order as the magnitudes they are related to are introduced in the book.

Before we start, note that some of the commands we will discuss are what Excel calls "arrays." For our purposes, the only important thing you need to know about them is that after typing the relevant expression, instead of hitting "Enter" you need to hit "Ctrl+Shift+Enter" *simultaneously.*

In order to illustrate the use of the commands we will discuss, it may be helpful to consider some figures. To that purpose, Exhibit A.1 shows the arithmetic (or simple) returns of two hypothetical assets, A and B. You may want to enter these returns in a spreadsheet, in the same cells as they are shown in the exhibit, to double check that you can implement the commands introduced, and obtain the results, reported below.

You can enter all the commands discussed from this point on in any empty cell of your spreadsheet. Logarithmic (or continuously compounded) returns can

Exhibit A.1

	A	B	C
1	**Period**	**Asset A**	**Asset B**
2	1	5%	-3%
3	2	12%	8%
4	3	-2%	6%
5	4	14%	15%
6	5	-6%	5%
7	6	5%	31%
8	7	11%	14%
9	8	-9%	-2%
10	9	15%	10%
11	10	7%	6%

be calculated with the "**LN**" function. To calculate the log return of asset A in period 1, you type

- =LN(1+B2)

hit "Enter," and you should obtain 4.9%.

Multiperiod arithmetic returns can be calculated with the "**PRODUCT**" array. To calculate the 10-period return of asset A, you type

- =PRODUCT(1+B2:B11) – 1

hit "Ctrl+Shift+Enter" simultaneously, and you should obtain 61.2%. Note that you can also obtain this same figure by considering log returns. In this case, you first calculate all ten log returns for asset A in cells D2 through D11, then type

- =EXP(SUM(D2:D11)) – 1

hit "Enter," and you should obtain the same 61.2%. Note that the "**SUM**" function simply adds up the ten log returns, and the "**EXP**" function raises the number e (=2.71828) to that sum.

You can also use these commands to calculate the value of an investment at the end of any holding period. To calculate the terminal value of $100 invested in Asset A at the beginning of Period 1, passively held through the end of Period 10, you can type

- =100*PRODUCT(1+B2:B11)

and hit "Ctrl+Shift+Enter" simultaneously; or you can type

- =100*EXP(SUM(D2:D11))

and hit "Enter". Either way, you should obtain $161.2.

Arithmetic mean returns can be calculated with the "**AVERAGE**" function. To calculate the arithmetic mean return of Asset A, you type

- =AVERAGE(B2:B11)

hit "Enter," and you should obtain 5.2%. Geometric mean returns, in turn, can be calculated with the "**GEOMEAN**" array. To calculate the geometric mean return of Asset A, you type

- =GEOMEAN(1+B2:B11) − 1

hit "Ctrl+Shift+Enter" simultaneously, and you should obtain 4.9%.

A dollar-weighted mean return, remember, is simply the IRR of the cash flows put into and obtained from an investment, so we will come back to this magnitude shortly when we discuss the implementation of the NPV and IRR concepts.

The standard deviation of returns can be calculated with the "**STDEVP**" function. To calculate the standard deviation of returns of asset A, you type

- =STDEVP(B2:B11)

hit "Enter," and you should obtain 8.0%. This magnitude can also be calculated with the "**STDEV**" function, which differs from the "STDEVP" function only in that the latter divides the sum of squared deviations from the mean by T (the number of observations) and the former by $T - 1$. Given that in finance we usually deal with large samples, this distinction is largely irrelevant. But if the number of observations is small, as is the case with the very small sample we are considering, then the difference may be less than negligible. To illustrate, if you calculate the standard deviation of returns of Asset A with the "STDEV" function, you should get 8.4% instead of the 8.0% calculated with the "STDEVP" function.

The beta of an asset can be calculated with the "**LINEST**" function. Because beta measures volatility relative to the market, assume that Asset B in Exhibit A.1 represents the returns of the market. In that case, to calculate the beta of Asset A, you type

- =LINEST(B2:B11, C2:C11)

hit "Enter," and you should obtain 0.35.

The correlation between the returns of two assets can be calculated with the "**CORREL**" function. To calculate the correlation between the returns of Assets A and B, you type

- =CORREL(B2:B11, C2:C11)

hit "Enter," and you should obtain 0.41.

Excel does not offer a built-in command to calculate semideviations. However, they can be calculated step by step as discussed in Tool 6; or in just one cell but with a rather cumbersome expression. Suppose you first calculate the arithmetic mean return of Asset A in cell B12; then, to calculate the semideviation with respect to that mean return, you type

- =SQRT(SUMPRODUCT(IF(B2:B11<B12, B2:B11 – B12, 0), IF(B2:B11<B12, B2:B11 – B12, 0))/10)

hit "Ctrl+Shift+Enter" simultaneously, and you should obtain 6.2%. As you can see, this expression makes use of the "**SQRT**" and "**IF**" functions and the "**SUMPRODUCT**" array. (The "IF" function serves the purpose of calculating the "conditional returns" as defined in Tool 6; the "SUMPRODUCT" array squares those "conditional returns"; and the "SQRT" function simply takes the square root of the average of "conditional squared returns.")

Note that the "10" by the end of the expression above is the number of observations in our sample but, more generally, you should input the number of observations of whatever sample you consider. An alternative is to replace the "10" by "**COUNT**(B2:B11)," which is a function that simply counts the number of observations in the range indicated.

Note, also, that as discussed in Tool 6, the semidevia- tion can be calculated with respect to *any* benchmark. Therefore, if instead of calculating the mean return in cell B12 you input any other magnitude (a target return, a risk-free rate, an expected rate of inflation, 0, or any other value of your interest), you can still use the same expression above.

Consider now Exhibit A.2. As before, you may find it helpful to input these figures in a spreadsheet, in the same cells as they are shown in the exhibit, to double check that you can implement the commands discussed and obtain the results reported below.

The net present value (NPV) of a project can be cal- culated with the "**NPV**" function. Importantly, note that Excel assumes that the first cash flow is one period away. In other words, if there is a current cash flow to be considered, *it must be added* to Excel's NPV calcula- tion. Note, also, that this calculation requires that you to input the discount rate, which means that you must assume or calculate this magnitude before you use the "NPV" function.

Exhibit A.2

	A	B	C	D	E	F
1	Period	Panel A		Panel B		Panel C
2		CF	Price	Passive	Active	CF
3	0	-$500	$50	-$5,000	-$5,000	-$950
4	1	$220	$55	$0	$0	$50
5	2	$240	$45	$0	-$4,500	$50
6	3	$310	$60	$0	$0	$50
7	4	$350	$70	$7,000	$14,000	$1,050

Panel A of Exhibit A.2 shows the cash flows (CF) of a hypothetical project that requires a $500 million investment today and is expected to generate the cash flows shown (all in millions) over the next four periods. Assume that the appropriate discount rate for this project is 10%. Then, to calculate the NPV of this project, you type

- =B3+NPV(0.1, B4:B7)

hit "Enter," and you should obtain $370.3 million. Note that the current cash flow (the $500 million initial investment in cell B3) is added to Excel's NPV calculation. Note, also, that "0.1" is the appropriate discount rate for the cash flows of this project, which you should replace with the appropriate discount rate for whatever project you consider.

The IRR of a project can be calculated with the "**IRR**" function. Importantly, note that unlike the "NPV" function, the "IRR" function assumes that the first cash flow takes place today. Therefore, to calculate the IRR of our project, you simply type

- =IRR(B3:B7)

hit "Enter," and you should obtain 38.0%.

The "IRR" function is also useful for the calculation of two other magnitudes discussed in this book, the dollar-weighted mean return and the yield to maturity. Panel B of Exhibit A.2 shows the prices of an asset and the cash flows of two investors in this asset. The first investor follows a passive strategy and simply buys 100 shares of the asset today (thus taking $5,000 out of his pocket) and sells them at the end of the fourth period (thus putting $7,000 into his pocket). The second investor follows a more active strategy, and, besides buying 100 shares today, he buys another 100 shares at the end of the second period (thus taking an additional $4,500 out of his pocket), and finally sells all 200 shares at the end of the fourth period (thus putting $14,000 into his pocket).

To calculate the dollar-weighted mean return of these two investors, you type

- =IRR(D3:D7)
- =IRR(E3:E7)

hit "Enter," and you should obtain 8.8% and 13.3%. (Recall that because the first investor follows a passive strategy, his dollar-weighted mean return and the asset's geometric mean return must be the same. You can double-check this yourself by calculating the asset's returns and then the geometric mean of those returns.)

The "IRR" function can also be used to calculate a bond's yield to maturity. Panel C of Exhibit A.2 shows the cash flows (CF) of a four-year bond with a face value of $1,000, an interest rate of 5%, and paying annual coupons. The first cash flow (–$950) is the current price of the bond preceded by a negative sign. Although a price obviously cannot be lower than 0, the negative cash flow indicates that if we buy this bond today we would have to take $950 *out* of our pocket. To calculate the yield to maturity of this bond, you type

- =IRR(F3:F7)

hit "Enter," and you should obtain 6.5%.

Exhibit A.3 summarizes the commands briefly discussed in this Appendix. You can get more information about all these commands in Excel's detailed help.

Exhibit A.3

LN	LINEST
PRODUCT (Array)	CORREL
EXP	SQRT
SUM	IF
AVERAGE	SUMPRODUCT (Array)
GEOMEAN (Array)	COUNT
STDEVP	NPV
STDEV	IRR

Index